# TAOISM

### and the
## RITE of COSMIC RENEWAL

SECOND EDITION

# TAOISM
## and the
## RITE of COSMIC RENEWAL

### SECOND EDITION

## Michael R. Saso

WSU
PRESS

Washington State University Press
Pullman, Washington
1990

Washington State University Press, Pullman, Washington 99164-5910

Printed and bound in the United States of America

99 98 97 96 95 94 93 92 91 90   10 9 8 7 6 5 4 3 2 1


Library of Congress Cataloging-in-Publication Data

Saso, Michael R.
  Taoism and the rite of cosmic renewal.

  Bibliography: p. 143
  1. Taoism. I. Title.
  BL1920.S27 1989   299'.51438   89-5687
  ISBN 0-87422-054-8(pbk)

# CONTENTS

# Preface to the First Edition

The purpose of *Taoism and the Rite of Cosmic Renewal* is to provide for the student of Asian religions a brief introduction to the ritual of orthodox Taoism, a topic about which little has been written in Western languages. Credit must be given to the Heavenly Master sect Taoist *Chuang-ch'en Teng-yün*, whose ritual performances are described in the following pages. Acknowledgements must especially be made to John Levy of London, through whose kindness and patience the research during the autumn and winter of 1969 was carried out. The trip to Chung-kang ward, Chunan city, north Taiwan, during November and December of 1970 was made possible through a grant from the graduate school of Washington State University, for which I am deeply grateful to Robert Boord, C. J. Nyman, and Allan Smith. Finally, the manuscript was typed and partially edited by Geneva Burkhart, and polished, refined, and edited by Henry Grosshans, whose many hours of labor made the work more readable and less imperfect. For the errors and inaccuracies, I take full responsibility.

There are many aspects of religious Taoism not touched upon in this book, and many mentioned but passed over for a second work, now under revision. The Taoist teachings of *Chuang-ch'en*, deriving from Lung-hu Shan in Kiangsi province, Wu-tang Shan in Hupei, and the Chi-yün monastery in Shensi I have made the theme of another book, where many of the subjects brought up in the present work are treated more fully. The relationships of the *Ho-t'u* and the *Lo-shu* to the training and the rank of a Taoist are here only briefly mentioned. Nothing is said of the age of the *Ho-t'u*, and citation is made of a cryptic passage in the *Wei Shu* apocrypha describing the *Ling-pao* Five Talismans as a kind of *Ho-t'u*. These topics are touched upon in the present work, which must be taken only as a basic introduction to a most difficult and complicated subject. It was the wish of the Taoist *Chuang-ch'en*, in revealing and explaining the rites described in the following pages, that they be somehow preserved and recorded in an age no longer convinced of their worth or meaning. It is with the hope that others more gifted and worthy than myself may turn to a study of religious Taoism and its ritual that the following pages are presented.

**MICHAEL R. SASO**

# Introduction to the First Edition

In December, 1970, while on a field trip in Taiwan, I was invited to take part in a village festival of renewal called *Chiao*.[1] The *Chiao*, which occurs in every village and city of Taiwan over a cycle of approximately sixty years, is traditionally performed by a Taoist priest and his entourage of disciples and musicians. In this instance, the priest hired to perform the ceremonies of renewal, a man in his mid-sixties named *Chuang-ch'en Teng-yün*, invited me to be present in order to photograph and record the proceedings. In 1971 I discussed the ceremonies in a series of lectures at Washington State University. The present study, based largely upon those lectures, makes available to the public for the first time the intricacies and the beauties of the esoteric rites of orthodox Taoism, an age-old ritual performed behind the locked doors of the village temple.

I do not intend, however, simply to present a series of pictures with extended explanations. Rather, I am primarily interested in showing the necessary connection of Chinese religion and Taoism, a connection whereby Taoism appears as a force which orders and gives theological meaning to the religion of the Chinese people. The good things which a Taoist attempts to acquire for himself, in the form of private meditation, rewards which include heaven's blessing, control over the spirits which cause sickness and suffering, and longevity, he also shares with the village community through public ritual and liturgy. The Taoist is himself a devout believer in the religion of the Chinese people, and as such performs the role in the community of expert in religious affairs. He is called upon to act as mediator with the invisible world of the spirits and demons who rule nature. He helps in the curing of sickness, and in winning blessings for the community. Finally, he is sometimes called upon to bury the dead, an unenviable role, which sets him apart from the ordinary society of men and women among whom he lives and labors.

The first chapter of this study describes the annual cycle of events in the religious and social life of a Chinese town or city. In the second chapter, I examine the *Chiao* festival as the villagers see it, a description which the anthropologist would call "etic," in that it is an external observer's view and does not enter into the esoteric theological explanations of the expert, the Taoist priest.   The third chapter attempts to show something of the "theology" of the *Chiao* festival, by quoting from early Taoist works and classical sources. The fourth chapter gives an "emic" or inside description of the *Chiao* festival, as the Taoist and his entourage witness it. Finally, the fifth chapter is devoted exclusively to the Taoists themselves, describing their various ranks and orders, the lists of gods, the *mudras* and *mantras*, which the Taoist must know in order to function. The last section of the book, following the Confucian dictum that a picture is worth a thousand words, presents a series of illustrations showing the visible aspects of what was described in chapter four. The incredibly complicated *Chiao* rituals will be seen to contain elements from feudal China, as well as rubrics dating from the beginnings of religious Taoist movements at the end of the Han dynasty, ca. 140-185 A.D.

By way of introduction, a word must be said about Taoism and the Taoist priest. Taoism is a term with many connotations. In its most widely known sense, it refers to a philosophy or a school of philosophers called *Tao Chia*, "School Taoism" in Chinese. In the philosophical sense the word "Taoism" calls to mind two famous men of feudal China, *Lao-tzu* and *Chuang-tzu*, whose works, or works ascribed to them, have frequently been translated into Western languages. The philosophical aspect of Taoism is considered to be mystical, passive, intellectual, the refuge of the literati who have fallen out of favor with the imperial court.[2]

In another sense, Taoism refers to a religious movement called *Tao Chiao*, "Church Taoism" or "Taoist Teachings" in Chinese.[3] Under the general heading of *Tao Chiao* can be included such diverse topics as alchemy, yoga, magic, meditation, and religious rituals performed for the sake of the devout believers in Chinese religion, the residents of China's countryside, towns, and cities. Taoists, or people who profess belief in religious Taoism, can perform a very wide range of functions. There are celibate or monastic Taoists who live in the great monastic centers on the mainland of China and practice meditation and self-perfection. There are popular Taoist priests called *Tao-shih* or "Taoist Masters," who live in the towns and cities of China, marry, and bear children. These men are also called "fire-dwelling" Taoists because they live by the fireside and help men over the difficult stages of life, providing ritual for the "Rites of Passage." They help cure sickness, ease childbirth, read prayers of blessings for marriage and for rain, and finally are called upon to bury the dead. They, therefore, perform an essential service for the communities in which they live. Their great "moment of truth," the summation of their lives as Taoist priests, comes at the village festival of renewal called *Chiao*, when they are called upon to perform their ancient rites behind the locked doors of the village temple. It is with such Taoists and the festival of renewal called *Chiao* that I am primarily concerned.

There are also lay Taoists, called *Hsin-shih* or believers, who study the meditations of the monastic Taoists, and try to abide by the principles of Taoist monastic life, though living in the world of everyday life and public affairs. The *Lung-men* bookshop in Taipei city is run by such an organization of men, who derive their name from the famous *Lung-men* sect on the mainland, which governed many monasteries around Nanjing and throughout Kiangsu province in China. Of the three classes of Taoist, monastic, "fire-dwelling" priest, and layman, the point must be stressed that their purposes and goals are theoretically identical. A Taoist is by belief a man or woman who attempts to attain immortality in the present life, so that on death he or she may be "wafted up to the realm of the immortals in broad daylight." The purpose of the monastic meditations, the public rituals, and the reading and meditating on esoteric books by laymen is the inner purification of the whole body, and each of the organs of the body, to the state of "Pure *Yang*," or life which does not pass away.

Unlike the process of nature, where everything passes from life to death, light to darkness, spring and summer to autumn and winter, the Taoist approach seeks to reverse the direction and to allow the Taoist to pass from death to life, from *Yin* to *Yang*, to the eternal state of a newborn child, ruddy, *Ch'ang-sheng*, i.e., "eternally being born anew." I will attempt to show how this process is accomplished and how it is defined. A Taoist is by definition a man who seeks immortality in the present life, rather than wait for the cleansing, purifying fires of the next life after death. It is not so much a longevity whereby man does not die but a state wherein he does not descend to the punishments of a fiery underworld after death that the Taoist seeks. What the monastic Taoist does by meditation, the fire-dwelling Taoist does through liturgy. The effects of longevous meditation are achieved through the performance of liturgy, given to the entire community.

Religious Taoism played a complicated part in the history of China. The origin of Taoism as a church is ascribed to two movements which occurred at the end of the Han dynasty, between 140 and 185 A.D. The first of these movements flourished in China's central provinces and called itself the Great

Peace movement.[4] Its leaders termed themselves Lords of Heaven, Earth, and Man, names which will be seen to bear religious significance in present-day Taoism, but which brought about a political upheaval in the years 184 and 185. The leaders of the movement and their immediate followers were considered subversive, and were destroyed in a series of campaigns ending in 185 A.D. Historians later renamed the movement the Yellow Turban Rebellion, due to the yellow cloths which the armies of followers wore around their heads.

The second movement called itself the Heavenly Master sect and was popular in China's western provinces, mainly in Szechuan and a part of Shensi. Father, son, and grandson named, respectively, *Chang Ling*, *Chang Heng*, and *Chang Lu*, were leaders of the new religious body; they established a spiritual and political system based upon the Han dynasty village administration. The village official called Wine-Libationer or *Chi-chiu* was made head of the parish, with a series of minor officials under him, duplicating the system found at the time throughout parts of China.[5] The term continues in use today, and many of the village Taoists include the word *Chi-chiu* in their title.[6] Unlike their brothers in the east-central plains of China, members of the Heavenly Master sect did not find it wise to oppose the central government. *Chang Lu*, the founder's grandson, surrendered to the conquering forces of *Ts'ao Ts'ao* at the end of the Han, and became established in Szechuan and Shensi as leader of a legitimate movement at the beginning of the Wei period, ca. 208-220 A.D. Historians refer to the movement as the Five Bushels of Rice thieves, because converts and adherents were taxed five bushels of rice. The fourth-generation descendant, according to legend, was supposed to have moved to Lung-hu Shan (Dragon-Tiger Mountain) in Kiangsi province, south China, from where the head of the *Cheng-i* Heavenly Master sect claimed descent until recent times.[7]

The origins of religious Taoism have, in fact, been traced much further back in history than the Heavenly Master sect and the Great Peace movement at the end of the Han. The reports of infamous court magicians called *Fang-shih*, whom *Ssu-ma Ch'ien* described in the *Shih Chi* (Historical Annals), the accounts of the early Han dynasty in the compilation of *P'an Ku*, and the description of the magic talismans which *Yü* the Great used to control the floods, found in the *Yüeh Chueh Shu*[8] (History of the Destruction of the Yüeh Kingdom), have been used by sinologists to describe the antecedents to what is known today as religious Taoism. Perhaps the most famous work on the origin of Taoism and of its priesthood is the sixth volume of De Groot's *The Religious System of China*. De Groot compares the

Taoist priests of Amoy at the end of the nineteenth century with the *Wu* and *Chu* exorcists of late Chou China.[9]

More germane to my presentation are the various themes and rituals which the Taoist makes use of in his role of ritual functionary for the believers in the Chinese religion. Three dominant themes can be found in the ritual meditations which the Taoist performs. The first theme is the ministry of exorcism and curing, perhaps the most fundamental and primitive of his tasks. The Taoist is called upon to cure sickness, and to expel the evil spirits which cause distress. This first and most ancient of his functions is ascribed to the special patronage of Lord *Lao*, or *Lao-tzu*, who is the third of a Taoist trinity, and patron of the third section of the Taoist canon. The ancient term for the style of liturgy and the lists of spirits, talismans, and formulae for this lowest but most important part of Taoist liturgy is *Meng-wei Ching-Lu* (the Auspicious Alliance Canonical Register). The historical accounts of the Heavenly Master sect's origins describe how the converts were made to write their sins on three documents, one addressed to the heavens, one to the earth, and one to the underworld realm of spirits. If a cure was not effected, the person was accused of being an insincere convert. Unsure as the biased accounts of the Confucian historian are, the theme of curing sickness by talismanic documents addressed to the three regions or realms of spirits is still to be found in modern Taoism.

A second theme consistently found throughout the history of religious Taoism is the performance of classical orthodox ritual, similar in some details to the rituals found in the *Book of Rites*, especially in the Monthly Commands chapter. The beginnings of the ministry of classical ritual found in the *Ling-pao Chen Wen* (the *Ling-pao* True Writs) and the *Ling-pao Wu-fu* (the *Ling-pao* Five Talismans) are present in the early apocryphal works of the Han dynasty called *Wei Shu*, Apocrypha, or "Woof" texts as contrary to and distinct from the *Ching* or "Warp," the classical Confucian tradition.[10] To the Taoist the liturgical *Ling-pao* tradition is thus seen as an ancient theme, separate from the Confucian tradition, but at the same time complementary to it as woof is to warp of a complete fabric. The Taoists assign the second person of a Taoist trinity, the *Ling-pao* Heavenly Worthy, as special patron of this tradition, mediator between heaven and earth, *i.e.*, liaison between the gods of the Prior Heavens and the posterior visible world. The second or liturgical part of the Taoist canon derives from the *Ling-pao*. The *Chiao* ritual in its present form can be found in the liturgical parts of the Taoist canon, dating from the fourth and fifth centuries of our era.[11] Its use as a complete liturgical form can be proved as continuous from almost the beginning of religious Taoism.

The third and perhaps most esoteric theme of religious Taoism is that of ritual meditation. This part of the Taoist tradition is the least known, and its origins are most difficult to unravel. The cryptic commentary of the Han dynasty, *Ts'an T'ung Ch'i* (Talisman of the Three Receptacles), which is credited to the Han recluse *Wei Po-yang*,[12] is thought to be the source of the meditative tradition, which was afterwards reformulated by another cryptic work, the *Huang-t'ing Ching* or *Yellow Court Canon*.[13] In dealing with the *Yellow Court Canon*, the Taoist tradition finds itself on firmer ground, since the historical origins of the work are more readily identifiable with Taoism. The name appears in the list of Taoist books compiled by *Ko Hung*, an eccentric who lived in the third century A.D. and compiled a two-volume work of Taoist lore called the *Pao-p'u-tzu*.[14] A short time later, the formidable lady Taoist *Wei Hua-ts'un* received the *Yellow Court Canon* from the spirit of *Wei Po-yang*, in a vision wherein a host of heavenly spirits revealed Taoist secrets. The *Yellow Court Canon* was systematically explained in thirty-nine sections in another work called the *Ta-tung Chen Ching*,[15] and these two works become the basis for the forming of the third great Taoist tradition, the theme of monastic meditation. The son of *Wei Hua-ts'un* and a recluse named *Yang Hsi*, living atop Mao Shan near Nanjing, in Kiangsu province, central China, become friends. In the fourth century of our era, the famous Mao Shan monastic center was organized by *Yang Hsi* and *Hsü Mi*, with eight monasteries for men and three for women. Meditation or "Internal Alchemy" was practiced by the Mao Shan sect on the lines of the *Yellow Court Canon*. The first of the Taoist trinity, the Primordial Heavenly Worthy, was considered patron of the tradition. The first part of the Taoist canon was likewise assigned as the receptacle for the teachings of the *Mao Shan* or the *Shang-ch'ing* (Highest Purity) order. The three traditions within the movements of early religious Taoism were thus complete.

It would be wrong, however, to think of the three traditions as exclusive. All three themes, curing, orthodox ritual, and meditation, were practiced by all Taoists. I will attempt to make the three themes clear, and to expand somewhat on their meaning. Though sinologists have traditionally made a distinction between monastic and popular "fire-dwelling" Taoists, all three of the above themes will be seen to be represented in each individual Taoist. The Taoists of Taiwan, whose rituals are described in the following pages, fulfill the ministry of exorcism and curing, perform the orthodox classical liturgy during the village festival of renewal called *Chiao*, and meditate according to the traditions of the *Yellow Court Canon*.

During and after the Sung dynasty Taoism grew and proliferated to include not three but five different themes, and thus divided into five distinct kinds of Taoists. In brief, the five kinds of Taoists recognized since the Sung, as defined by the ordination manual of the 61st-generation Heavenly Master of Lung-hu Shan in 1859, in a manuscript discovered by the author on Taiwan, are as follows:[16]

1. The *Yü-ching* sect. The *Mao Shan* Taoists, who base their life and their meditative ritual on the *Yellow Court Canon.*

2. The *T'ien-shu* sect. The *Ch'uan-chen* and the *Lung-men* Taoists, who live much as Buddhist monks, with celibacy and vegetarianism as strict rules of life. The sect was founded during the Sung dynasty.

3. The *Pei-chi* or Pole Star Taoists. The home of the order is Wu-tang Shan in Hupei. The Sung dynasty saw a development of exorcistic and militaristic ritual at this famous center, which eventually became the object of the patronage of Ming dynasty emperors. The claimed origins of the order are from the Han dynasty, the famous general *Chu-ko Liang,* and militaristic ritual such as is found in the *Pa-ch'en T'u,* and the *Ch'i-men Tun-chia.*[17] The spirits of the Pole Star, efficacious in exorcising evil, are summoned and controlled through the registers and frenzied ritual of the order.

4. The *Yü-fu* or Jade Pavilion sect. The term refers to the orthodox Heavenly Master sect of Lung-hu Shan in Kiangsi. Taoists belonging to this order are called Black-head on Taiwan. Their ritual and practices are the main subject of my discussion.

5. The *Shen-hsiao* order. A heterodox group of Taoists who flourished during the Hsüan-ho reign from 1119 to 1126. The order was considered heterodox because it originated from Lu-Shan in Kiangsi, a mixed Buddhist-Taoist center, and developed rituals which made use of mediums, possessions, and other disapproved forms of magic, as well as the more orthodox rituals of the Heavenly Master sect. The order is generally termed "Red-head" by the People of Taiwan, referring not to a red cloth or headdress, but to the fact that these Taoists do not usually bury the dead.

Though elements of all five kinds of Taoists appear in my account, only the last two orders, namely the Black-head and the Red-head (that is, the *Yü-fu* and the *Shen-hsiao* orders), are to be found on Taiwan. The avowed purpose of the Taoist, and the end sought by his meditations and ascetic life, is purification and refinement of the body, so that upon death he will be wafted up to heaven in broad daylight, and live the life of an immortal. Longevity, defined as *Hsien*-hood or immortality after death, is in fact only paid lip-service by the Black-head and Red-head Taoists of Taiwan. The profession of being a "fire-dwelling" Taoist, assisting at exorcisms, curing illness, burying the dead, and performing at temple rituals including the lengthy *Chiao* ritual of renewal, obscures the esoteric and lofty ideals of traditional ascetic Taoist life. The village Taoist is a man who drinks, who is feared by his neighbors for his strange profession of speaking with the gods, and who often must depend on some other profession in order to live. Only the Black-head Taoists who bury the dead can actually make a living in their profession, a living which is meager enough, often bringing but a small stipend for late-night rituals, or the accompanying of the coffin on its procession to the grave in the heat of midday. The Taoist's profession is neither easy nor enviable.

It is only at the great *Chiao* ritual of renewal that he can assume some of the glories of his past, and fulfill for a few days the role of wine-libationer for the community of believers. It is on this specific occasion, that is, the *Chiao* festival of renewal during which time the Taoist is called upon to perform the rites of orthodox Taoism, that the present work will focus. The relationship of the Taoist to the popular religion will appear to be basic. Such a study, in addition to providing a description of factual events that accompany village ritual, will indicate the relationship between Taoism and Chinese popular religion. Perhaps it will also shed some light on a despised and little-known role, that of the hidden village Taoist, whose ritual duties may soon be forgotten in a modern China turning more and more to science and rejecting the traditional past. One is reminded of the theme stated by Joseph Needham in his monumental *Science and Civilisation in China:*[18] it was the Taoist, after all, who preserved the spirit of science in China, against the pen of the literati in the Confucian tradition, whose hands were never soiled by physical labor. The Taoist always chose to remain hidden and unknown. His rituals were and are performed behind the locked doors of the village temple. When revealed, at last, for public appraisal, perhaps the role of the Taoist in Chinese cultural tradition will be given a more deserving and respectful place.

# Introduction to the Second Edition

I am grateful to the Washington State University Press, which has graciously allowed me to write an update of chapter five and an introduction to this second edition. Work on the original manuscript of *Taoism and the Rite of Cosmic Renewal* began in 1964, when I first attended the *Chiao* festivals of the Red-head Taoists of Hsinchu and T'ao-yüan counties, Taiwan, under the tutelage of Master *Ch'ien*, whose picture appears in the photo section included herein. Later, through the introduction of the wood-carver *Su* and others, I was admitted into the entourage of *Chuang-ch'en Teng-yün*, whose Black-head *Cheng-i Meng-wei* style *Chiao* liturgy is described here and in my book, *The Teachings of Taoist Master Chuang* (New Haven, 1978).

Recently, through the kindness of *Huang Ch'eng-feng* and *Lai Yung-hai* of Nanjing University, I was allowed for the first time to visit various centers of Taoist activity in the People's Republic of China between May 1987 and August 1988. During these surveys, I found deep and convincing proof of the hypotheses presented by Master *Chuang*, *i.e.*, (1) that Taoist liturgy acts out the philosophy of *Lao-tzu* and *Chuang-tzu*, and (2) the *Cheng-i Meng-wei* style of *Chiao* celebrated by *Chuang* is structurally modeled on the meditations of internal alchemy. These findings are incorporated in the revised chapter five.

The religious traditions described here are common to mainland and Taiwanese Taoists who follow the Three Mountain Drop of Blood Alliance ( *San-shan Ti-hsüeh P'ai*) shortened to Three Mountain Alliance for convenience. The three mountains referred to in this title are in mainland China: Lung-hu Shan (Dragon-Tiger Mountain) and Ko-tsao Shan in Kiangsi province, and Mao Shan in Kiangsu province. The Mao Shan complex, sixty kilometers southeast of Nanjing, is perhaps the most famous Taoist mountain in China. Its caves and pine-covered hills have attracted Taoist recluses since pre-Ch'in times (before 221 B.C.). It is occupied by the *Shang-ch'ing*

(Highest Pure) order of meditating Taoists. Lung-hu Shan, on the other hand, has been considered the headquarters of the Celestial Master *Chang T'ien-shih* and the *Cheng-i Meng-wei* style of liturgy from the mid Sung dynasty onward (ca. 1000-1100 A.D.). It is this style of *Chiao* liturgy that is practiced by *Chuang* and the Taoists of north Taiwan. The third mountain complex, Ko-tsao Shan, is traditionally considered to be the center of *Ling-pao San-wu Tu-kung* style liturgy, as practiced by the Taoists of Tainan city, south Taiwan. From the Sung dynasty onward (960-1281 A.D.), these three centers were appointed by the Imperial Court to examine and license Taoists to perform rituals according to an approved canonical tradition. The licenses and *Lu* or registers that list what a Taoist is allowed to do in the way of meditation, liturgy, and so forth are contained in a manual called *San-shan Ti-hsüeh P'ai* (The Three Mountain Drop of Blood Alliance). It has been published in my collection of Taoist esoterica entitled *Dokyo Hiketsu Shusei* (Tokyo, 1979).

From the manual we can clearly see that the highest rank of ordination is given to a Taoist who knows how to conduct the *Yellow Court Canon* meditations of the Highest Pure order of Mao Shan. The next higher ranks are given to the masters who perform the Thunder meditations of a little known order called *Ch'ing-wei* (Pure Subtle). It was not until I climbed Mao Shan that I discovered the origin of this term. Mao Shan has three peaks named after three brothers who practiced meditation and healing there in the early Han dynasty (ca. 160-140 B.C.). *Ch'ing-wei* refers to Taoists of the second and third peak who practice a form of Thunder and Lightning meditation described in chapter six of my book, *The Teachings of Taoist Master Chuang*.

There are many kinds of Thunder rituals practiced by the Taoists of Taiwan in both the popular Red-head and classical Black-head styles of liturgy. The differences in these styles, revealed during my survey of mainland China, are described in the revised chapter five. Thus, knowledge of the *Ch'ing-wei* Thunder liturgy is the criterion for the second and third highest Taoist ordination title, whereas the *Cheng-i Meng-wei* style is ranked fourth and fifth, and the *Ling-pao* (Three-five Surveyor of Merit) titles are sixth and seventh. Informally, the eighth and ninth are Incense Master, and Procession Leader. There are in all nine ranks or titles, replicating the Confucian Imperial Mandarinate system. Thus, the nine ranks of Taoist priests are to the transcendent *Tao* what the nine grades of Confucian officials once were to the emperor.

The present work describes the *Chiao* liturgy of the *Cheng-i Szu-t'an* (Heirs to the *Cheng-i* Tradition) of Hsinchu city, north Taiwan. This tradition represents the teachings of *Cheng-i Meng-wei* Taoism as transmitted from Lung-hu Shan in Kiangsi province. Since the completion of *Taoism and the Rite of Cosmic Renewal* in 1972, a number of books have been written about the *San-wu Tu-kung* (Three-five Surveyor of Merit) *Chiao* ritual of the *Ch'en* clan of Tainan city, south Taiwan. Chapter five also takes note of these more recent publications based on the *Chiao* ritual of Master *Ch'en*. An early mimeographed report by Kristofer M. Schipper entitled "Taoism: The Liturgical Tradition," presented at the First International Conference on Religious Taoism, Bellagio, Italy (1968), was the first of many studies about this extremely different form of *Chiao*. John Lagerwey's *Taoist Ritual in Chinese Society and History* (New York, 1987), and Ofuchi Ninji's *Chugokujin no Shukyo Girei* [The Rituals of Chinese Religion] (Tokyo, 1983), present massive, detailed accounts of the Tainan Taoist rite. These works present an "etic" or external view of the *Ling-pao* Three-five Surveyor of Merit rites, with no mention of the meditations of internal alchemy. For this and other reasons, including the need to verify the use or nonuse of *Nei-tan* alchemical meditations in south Taiwan, I did not use materials from outside the Hsinchu area in the first edition, but cite them here should the reader have further interest. The work of Ofuchi, in particular, presents firsthand, detailed reporting with the original Chinese text quoted in part for verification.

The entire *Chiao* ritual of the *Cheng-i Meng-wei* Black-head and the *Shen-hsiao* Red-head traditions has been published in Chinese in my twenty-five volume *Chuang-lin Hsü Tao-tsang* [The Chuang-Lin Family Supplement to the Taoist Canon] (Taipei, 1975). The original texts cited here can be found in that collection.

These valuable manuscripts were preserved and transmitted by the Taoists of north Taiwan. Along with the materials published by Ofuchi, they can be used to verify the fact that the Taoists of Taiwan follow exactly the rituals shared with the Taoists of the Three Mountain Alliance of mainland China. In fact, the ritual tradition preserved in Taiwan actually is more complete than the texts preserved on the mainland. It is an important source for understanding the Taoist tradition throughout China and for restoring that tradition after the disruptions of the Cultural Revolution.

One point made in *Taoism and the Rite of Cosmic Renewal* is crucial for an understanding of Taoism as it is practiced in China. Many Westerners who have never been outside a modern, materialistic environment find Taoism of the popular paperback book market variety to be appealing. They perceive Taoism as allowing for freedom from form and ritual, release from rule and restriction, and development of the self to its fullest potential.

However, is the Tao of sex, like the Zen of motorcycling, a western product? Taoists in China, for instance, often do not eat meat, are celibate, and follow strict ascetic practices. Taoists believe in spirits, perform rituals, heal the sick, practice martial arts to expel evil, and bury the dead. The answer to this question must be gleaned from historical study, field research, and personal experience. It is not enough to read an English translation of *Lao-tzu* or criticize a translation of a Chinese text without knowing the context and the hermeneutics (art of interpretation) used to translate it. Taoism in China is an oral (singing and dancing) and not a written tradition. The best English/Chinese dictionaries do not contain specialized Taoist terms. One must rely on the interpretation of the Taoist master for understanding the text at hand. For this reason, both this work and *The Teachings of Taoist Master Chuang* (especially chapters five and six of the latter work) contain interpretative, not literal, translations.

In this brief introduction, I can only begin to touch upon what the Taoists' oral traditions from Hsinchu of north Taiwan, Mao Shan in Kiangsu province, Lung-hu Shan in Kiangsi, and Chang-chou in Fukien province say about internal alchemy and the *Chiao*. For all of these traditions, the structure of the basic *Chiao* festival is the same. The five *Chiao* rites that I have called "C" (classic) style (the *Su-ch'i*, Morning, Noon, and Night Audiences, and the *Tao-ch'ang*) are for the Taoists of the Three Mountain Alliance, in fact, an expression of internal alchemy meditation. These rituals retrace the workings of the Transcendent *Tao* ( *Wu-wei Chih Tao*) in nature. The forty-second chapter of *Lao-tzu* states the basic premise:

The *Tao* ( *Wu-wei*) gives birth to the One ( *Yu-wei*, *Ch'i*-breath).
The One (breath) gives birth to the Two ( *Yang*, spirit).
The Two ( *Yang*) gives birth to the Three ( *Yin*, essence).
The Three ( *Ch'i-yang-yin*) give birth to the myriad creatures.

The principle of reversal (return to the *Tao*), the turn of the potter's wheel, and the seasonal cycle of nature are signs of the *Tao*'s eternal spinning out of this process. The purpose of Taoist ritual of the "C" theme, as described in chapter four, is to dramatically act out this procession. Here you will see that the *Yin-yang* five element theory plays a central role in Taoist philosophy and cosmology. Wood (3) and fire (2) are refined into *Yang* breath; metal (4) and water (1) are fused in fires of internal meditation into *Yin*. It is incumbent on the reader to see and hear the processes of nature symbolized in this meditation of renewal. Spring (green) and summer fire (red) are within the human body microcosm, where autumn's harvest (metal, white) and winter's cooling water (purple-blue) fill and renew.

Proceeding from words to symbolic colors is easy to understand. The further step from symbol to spirit is harder for the materialistic Western mind to envision. Here we must leave aside our prejudices for the wisdom of the Taoist masters. Beginning at the end of the Han period (ca. 145-215 A.D.), Taoists became the priests of China's folk religion, a choice due more to popular demand than Imperial favor. The human mentality of former times is hard for the modern "scientific" (observation-based) mind to comprehend. By the archaeology of the mind, we must dig out that strata that once identified the powers of nature with the invisible world of spirits. Rivers, trees, earth, sky, rain, sun, and moon are personified in folk religions. In this same manner, demons of anger, greed, and vengeance can be made to exist, and can be "cast out" with eidetic vision to restore mental health, a process approved by Jungian analysts. Some Taoists accepted the spirits as real in the psychological sense as projections of the imagination, while others perceived them in a literal or spiritual sense as actual beings to be ritually cajoled, expelled, or manipulated.

Some Taoists used the *Lao-tzu* and *Chuang-tzu* as meditative guides, while others deified *Lao-tzu* in a cult accepted into the system of Imperial Sacrifice: see, Anna Seidel, *La Divinisation de Lao-tseu dans le Taoïsme des Han* (Paris, 1969). The point to be made here is that Taoists of the *Cheng-i Meng-wei* and *Shang-ch'ing* Mao Shan traditions cast out or exorcise spirits before approaching union with the *Tao*.

In the spirit of *Chuang-tzu* ("Only *Tao* dwells in the void," *Chuang-tzu Nei-p'ien*, chapter four), the higher grades of meditating Taoists considered all visualization of spirits to be contrary to the meditations of kenosis or emptying performed during internal alchemy. The rites of the *Chiao* festival were therefore interpreted to be a dramatic acting out of the process of emptying and union. The expelling of the spirits took place during the *Fa-lu* rite for lighting an interior fire inside the body, *i.e.*, in the lower cinnabar field below the Yellow Court (microcosmic center) where union with the *Tao* takes place in ritual and in meditation. It is precisely in this regard, *i.e.*, the alchemy of emptying the microcosmic center, that the meditations of the Mao Shan *Shang-ch'ing* tradition differ from all other Taoists. Since this tradition is a part of the Three Mountain Alliance, it is shared by all Taoists who go above the Grade Six level ordination. The *Yellow Court Canon*, the text in which the emptying of spirits and union with the *Tao* is described, is chanted at midnight of the second day of the *Chiao*, on the night before the meditation of union, *Tao-ch'ang Cheng-chiao*, takes place. This new introduction to the second edition therefore adds this information to the earlier text. With the exception of the revised fifth chapter and a supplemental bibliography, this book remains otherwise unchanged. I apologize and take full blame for all errors and lack of clarity in past works, and hope that the spirit of Chinese Taoism in all of its many facets will shed light on all who read these pages.

# I

# The Yin-Yang Theory as the Basis of Chinese Religion

The principles from which Taoism derives, descending from the *Yin-Yang* five-element school of ancient Chinese philosophy, are the same basic principles that guide the Chinese religion. The plausibility of this hypothesis may be established by two sets of demonstrative materials. The first is based upon classical texts explaining the principles of the *Yin-Yang* five-element school; the second is of factual events showing that the rites and festivals of the popular religion are, in fact, based upon the principles of *Yin, Yang,* and the five elements. The relationship of the Taoist to the Chinese religion will be seen to be one of functionary expert. In the major rites of passage, in the daily needs and emergencies of the household, and finally in the great village festival of renewal, it is the Taoist who is called upon as consultant, and whose presence is needed to perform the necessary rituals.

In communities where a Taoist resides, the relationship between Taoism and the religion of China is more readily demonstrable than in those many parts of China and Taiwan where Taoists are scarce, or Buddhism prevails. As a general rule, proximity to a Buddhist monastery might lead to a conspicuous absence of Taoist priests and their ministry. The rituals offered in a Buddhist monastery, however, when patronized by devout adherents of Chinese religion, do not differ appreciably from similar rituals offered in a local temple, under the direction of a Taoist. In both cases the principles of the Chinese religion—principles based on the *Yin-Yang* five-element theory of the cosmos—are the crucial factors. Many eminent scholars have seen the importance of the *Yin-Yang* theory. Among the more basic works is C. K. Yang's *Religion in Chinese Society,* a clear and illuminating study. Laurence G. Thompson's *Chinese Religion: An Introduction* is an enlightened and masterful synthesis. The encyclopedic work of De Groot, *The Religious System of China,* is perhaps the most exhaustive work on the subject, going back into antiquity to discover the sources of modern Chinese religion.[1] I shall try to demonstrate that there is no Taoist who is not firstly a devout believer in the spirits, the ancestors, and the annual cycle of feasts and customs. The ends which he hopes to gain for himself by ritual meditation and self-discipline, he shares with the village community through the rituals of orthodox Taoism. When called upon to explain either the religious practices he performs or the cosmology of the Chinese religion, he draws upon the philosophical school of *Yin-Yang* and the five elements, the principles of which are contained in a manual given to him at the time of his ordination. The name of the manual is *Tao Chiao Yüan Liu* (The Origins of Religious Taoism).[2]

The *Yin-Yang* and the five-element schools were originally divergent theories which amalgamated, according to a commonly held opinion among modern sinologists, sometime toward the beginning of the Han dynasty (ca. 220 B.C.)[3] The classical works which are cited as representative of the school are the *Hung-fan* chapter of the *Book of History,* the *Po-hu T'ung,* a compilation of the "new text" philosophers of the early Han period, the commentary on the Spring-Autumn Annals by a scholar named *Lü,* the *Book of Rites,* and the *Huai-nan-tzu,* a Taoist work. The theory of *Yin-Yang* and the five elements later came to be the basis for the philosophy of the Neo-Confucian school, and was epitomized in the work called *T'ai-chi T'u-shuo* (Illustrated Explanation of the *T'ai Chi,* Great Ultimate) by *Chou Tun-i.* The Taoist's manual, the *Tao Chiao Yüan Liu,* cites passages from the above-mentioned work as pertinent to the training and requisite knowledge of the Taoist priest.

According to this literate tradition, affirmed and reaffirmed throughout the history of China's great thinkers, the cosmos is a series of progressions from the One Great Ultimate, the *T'ai Chi,* to the two principles, *Yin* and *Yang,* the three sources, heaven, earth, and man, the four seasons, five elements, eight trigrams, and so forth. From the combination of *Yin* and *Yang* the myriad creatures are produced.

The principle *Yang* is conceived to be the rule of heavens. It corresponds to light, fire, life, masculinity, and movement. The principle *Yin* is realized in the earth. It corresponds to darkness, water, death, femininity, and stillness. The two principles *Yin* and *Yang* divide to form the points of the compass. Winter correlates to the north, when *Yin* is at zenith and *Yang* is reborn. The winter solstice celebrates this event. Spring corresponds to the east and the color green when the world of nature is reborn. Summer matches with the south; *Yang* is at zenith and *Yin* is reborn. Finally, autumn and the west correspond to the setting sun, when nature has finished producing its crops for men and begins the long rest of winter.

The popular religion is not concerned with creation or protogenesis. It is geared to the needs of the common man, the changes in the seasons, planting, harvesting, and rest. The winter solstice, *i.e.*, the solar New Year, celebrates the rebirth of the principle of *Yang*. The sun, the Great *Yang* (*T'ai-yang*), begins to grow in strength. Its fiery life is reborn, causing nature to awaken. Man, on the other hand, passes from life to death, and is not reborn; only through his progeny does he continue his line, and is fed by his descendants' offerings in the unknown life of the netherworld. It was perhaps from such a knowledge of nature that the Taoist idea of rebirth originated. If one could imitate nature and hold in his grasp the principle of life and *Yang*, then the process from life to death could be reversed. *Yang*, instead of being replaced by *Yin*, could be restored; man might perhaps "return to his roots" and "restore the origin."[4] The Taoist was, therefore, very interested in the origin of the cosmos and the origin of the annual rebirth in nature. He drew upon the *Yin-Yang* five-element theory of the past to establish his own knowledge and grasp of rebirth in the universe.

The catechetical manual of the Taoist, the *Tao Chiao Yüan Liu* (The Origin of Taoism), does not speak of creation, but of generation. Before heaven and earth were divided there was simply a primordial undifferentiated mass called *Hun-t'un*. The mass seethed and churned until in the very center was formed a drop of primordial breath. The mass, before congealing, was the nameless primordial ultimate, the invisible transcendent principle, *Wu-chi*. The drop which congealed in the center was the visible, immanent "Great Ultimate," the *T'ai Chi*.[5]

The "Great Ultimate" moved, and gave birth to *Yang*. Having fulfilled its movement, it then rested, and gave birth to *Yin*. *Yin* and *Yang* then joined in a productive and harmonious union which gave birth to the five elements, in the following fashion:[6]

From the Great *Yang* comes water;
    Great *Yang* is prior to breath;
From the Great Beginning is born fire;
    The Great Beginning possesses breath but
    is prior to substance.
From the Great Origin comes wood;
    The Great Origin has form, but
    does not yet have material stuff.
From the Great Substance is born metal;
    The Great Substance possesses material stuff
    but does not yet have phenomenal aspect.
From the Great Ultimate is born earth
    Visible form and material substance are complete
    in the Great Ultimate [the *T'ai Chi*].

The above process is a foreshadowing of the productive activity of *Yin* and *Yang* that causes the five elements to give birth to each other. The production of the five elements is forecast in the fivefold stages from the transcendent ultimate *Wu-chi* to the visible immanent ultimate *T'ai-chi*. The process which precedes all transformational change in the visible world is itself a series of five changes, which takes place in the Prior Heavens. It is significant that the number is five, the basic number of the life-giving chart, the *Ho-t'u* that was used as a basis for Taoist ritual.

The five primordials can be found at every level of the macrocosm and the microcosm. They are to be found firstly in the Prior Heavens, the abode of the primordial breaths that caused protogenesis. They are also to be found in the earthly dimension embedded in the five sacred peaks of China. Finally, they are to be found in the microcosm within man, in the five central organs of the body. Just as the five virtues of benevolence, righteousness, loyalty, faith, and filial piety are basic to the doctrines of Confucianism, so the five elements are central to Taoism.[7]

The *Tao Chiao Yüan Liu*, quoting the *T'ai-chi T'u Shuo* of the Neo-Confucianist *Chou Tun-i*, describes the above notions in the following fashion:[8]

The *Wu-chi* gives birth to the *T'ai-chi*.
[The *T'ai-chi*] moves and gives birth to *Yang*.
Rests, and gives birth to *Yin*.
*Yang* shifts, *Yin* unites,
Then is born water, fire, wood, metal, and earth.
The *Five Breaths* make things flourish in their
    proper order;
The four seasons progress according to them.

Thus the seasons and all of the visible world are governed by the breaths of the five elements, which are spatial as well as temporal concepts. The element wood governs the spring, the east, and the liver within man. The element fire governs the summer, the direction south, and the heart of man. The element metal governs the west, the season autumn, and the lungs of man. The element water governs the north, the season winter, and the kidneys within man. Finally the element earth governs the center and the spleen within man.

The whole of man's body thus corresponds to the primordial workings of the Great Principle, *T'ai Chi, Yin* and *Yang*, and the five elements. When *Yin* and *Yang* divided, *Yang* being light went upward and formed the heavens. *Yin* being heavy descended and formed the earth.[9] Man's body also corresponds to this distinction; the head is the heavens, and the eyes are sun and moon.[10] In each of the parts of the body, corresponding to the structure of the universe, is a spirit. The five organs mentioned above have a ruling spirit. The left and right hands are official spirit messengers. The left and right feet hold the dragon and tiger lords. The upper parts of the body contain the *Yang* spirits of the heavens, and the lower parts hold the *Yin* spirits of earth. As the head represents heaven, so the feet are earth.

If the microcosm is a reflection of the macrocosm, then the principles of *Yin* and *Yang* must be at work within the body of man, just as they are at work in the universe. Man at birth, in the state of a ruddy, healthy child, is filled with the principle of primordial *Yang*, like the sun at the winter solstice. As he grows, *Yang* waxes until at maturity it has reached its peak. But *Yin* too is present, in germinal form within man. As life goes on, *Yin* increases, and *Yang* gradually flows away. Finally, at the moment of death, the balance of *Yin* and *Yang* is no longer effective, man's breath, spirit, and seminal essence are dissipated. Death is not a separation of body and spirit, as in the Western and especially the Platonic sense. It is rather a separation of the *Yang* and *Yin* parts of man, an understanding of which rests on the comprehension of the Chinese concept of soul.

To the believer in the Chinese religion as well as to the Taoist, the totality of man is, therefore, composite. The principles of *Yin* and *Yang* are the basis for this composition. The *Yin* part of man is conceived of as that part which returns to the soil upon death. The *Yang* part is that which wanders upward as a spirit.

De Groot quotes the *Li Yün* chapter of the *Li Chi* to the effect, "Man consists of the beneficial substances that compose the heavens and the earth, of the cooperation of *Yin* and *Yang*, and the union of a *Kuei* [demon] and a *Shen* [spirit]. He consists of the finest breath of the five elements."[11] The soul of man is composite. The *Yin* part of the soul is called *P'o*, a character composed of the word for demon and white. This part of the soul is also called *Kuei*, and it is the *Kuei* or *P'o* which returns to the earth upon death.[12]

The *Yang* part of the soul is called *Shen* or *Hun*. *Shen* means spirit, and the spirit is said to wander about as an orphan until an ancestor tablet is erected for it, or until it can be released to waft upward as a "Bright Spirit." De Groot again quotes the *Li Chi* from the *Chi Yi* chapter:[13]

The 'Ch'i breath' is the full manifestation of the *Shen*, and the *P'o* is the full manifestation of the *Kuei*. The union of the *Kuei* with the *Shen* is the highest of all tenets. Living beings are all sure to die, and as they certainly return to the earth after their death, the soul which accompanies them thither is called *Kuei*. But while the bones and flesh moulder in the ground and mysteriously become earth of the fields, the *Ch'i* issues forth and manifests itself on high as a shining *Ming* light.

There is, then, a threefold relationship among *Yang*, breath, and spirit, and among *Yin*, demon, and *P'o*. The name for the *Yang* part of man's soul before death is *Hun*, and after death is *Shen*. The term for the *Yin* part of the soul before death is *P'o*, and after death is *Kuei*. The gods in the Chinese temples are called *Shen-ming*, that is, "Bright Spirits," because they are spirits who have been wafted to the bright heavens, and have been vested with authority to grant blessing or punish men in the visible world.

Other gods of the folk religion are, in fact, demonic, although they are given the title *Shen* as a euphemism. In many cases they were human beings who died a violent death in the popular folklore accounts. Such demonic spirits are, for instance, the guardian gods of the Ch'eng Huang temple who haul unfortunate souls to the underworld for punishment. Also in this class are the gods of pestilence called *Wang Yeh* (Amoy dialect, *Ong-ia*). According to one of the many folklore accounts, the *Wang Yeh* were once mandarins in Fukien province. Walking along a country roadside, they came upon a well that had been cursed by a demon and was causing a plague in the countryside. To save the people from the plague, the mandarins threw themselves in the well, thus in dying saving the people from drinking the water.[14] In a frenzied ceremony performed by the Taoists, the *Wang Yeh* are expelled from the village precincts by being pushed out to sea in a boat, or by being burned in effigy.[15] The exorcism of the *Wang Yeh* protects the villagers from the ravages of sickness.

Another distinction between a *Kuei* or demon and a *Shen* or spirit is one of burial. The *Kuei* is a spirit which has not been properly returned to the earth, such as a person who died by drowning, or an "orphan soul" (*Ku-hun*) who has no ancestor tablet and no one to offer food or incense before the ancestor shrine. These harmful spirits, who seek vengeance on mankind for their unfortunate positions in the underworld, are collectively worshipped in out-of-the-way temples, and are considered to be the patrons of prostitutes and gamblers.[16]

The *P'o* part of man, the *Yin* soul, is traditionally divided into seven, and is said to control the passions. The *Hun* soul is divided into three, and produces the virtues. The lengthy passage of De Groot on the topic can be summarized in the following table.[17]

1.  *Yang* produces the *Hun*, which produces human nature, composed of:

| *Benevolence* | *Righteousness* | *Propriety* | *Wisdom* | *Faith* |
|---|---|---|---|---|
| Liver | Lungs | Heart | Kidneys | Spleen |
| Wood | Metal | Fire | Water | Earth |
| East | West | South | North | Center |
| Blue | White | Red | Black | Yellow |
| Eyes | Nose | Ears | Tubes | Mouth |
| Dragon | Tiger | Red Bird | Tortoise | Crucible |

2. *Yin* produces the *P'o*, which governs the passions:

Joy.........................West
Anger.....................East
Sorrow....................Nadir (*Hsia*)
Merriment..............Zenith (*Shang*)
Likes......................North
Dislikes.................South
Desire....................

In the above chart, the virtues produced by the *Yang* soul, the *Hun*, correspond to the five directions, the seasons, and the elements. One of the basic rituals of orthodox Taoism is to restore the primordial state of these organs in the microcosm, filling them with the spirits of the heavens, while removing the influence of the baleful demons of the underworld. Since the microcosm and the macrocosm correspond, the Taoist subsequently plants the same life-giving primordial breath into the five directions of the community village.[18]

If the principles of Chinese religion can be expressed in a clear and succinct manner, one can say that the purpose of the prayers, rituals, and other activities of the system is to win the blessing associated with *Yang* and suppress the evil forces belonging to *Yin*. In the minds of the men and women of the community, the power of good and evil, *Yang* and *Yin*, are personified into world after world and layer after layer of spirits, good and evil. The highest spirits, residents in heaven, are associated with life and blessing. The spirits who rule the visible world, such as the god of the hearth and the lord of the soil, watch over the good and evil deeds of men, reporting them to the heavenly rulers for reward or punishment. The demons of the underworld, both orphan souls and the spirits of men who died a death by violence, cause harm to men through sickness, calamity, and misfortune. Men and women of the visible world handle the spirits much as they handle the visible magistrates of the central government. The gods are banqueted and rewarded, thus building relationships of reciprocal obligation. Demons and spirits are given paper money as bribes, much as one buys political favor and influence. One can by burning paper money, toy houses, and other desired objects accumulate "merit" and "credit" in the invisible world of the spirits. Good deeds stemming from the principle of *Yang* add to the spiritual bank of merit; evil deeds stemming from *Yin*, passion, and violence act as negative factors and cause punishment in the afterlife in the netherworld.

When a member of the family is sick, one first asks a medium to identify the spirit which is displeased and is causing the illness. When a baby cries at night, incense and rice are offered to the mother goddess of the bed, who is supposed to make the baby stop crying. The granting of a favor by a god means that the family must fulfill a vow, either to buy a new silk gown to dress the effigy of the spirit in the temple, or sponsor a puppet show on the stage of the local temple in the god's honor. None of these acts is to be interpreted as naive superstition. Rather, they are socially oriented acts of filial piety and reciprocity; honoring one's parents in the visible world is related to the care and feeding of one's ancestors, just as favors and debts incurred must be repaid to men and spirits alike. A man of virtue acts toward the gods as he does to his fellowmen. The man who acts generously as does heaven, repaying gifts freely received from the heavenly deities, will, in turn, be rewarded by society and the spirits for his magnanimous sense of sharing. A man who gives generously to the temple for public festivals fulfills one of the requirements for leadership in the village community.[19]

There are various functionaries called upon to perform the rites of Chinese religion. The first and foremost of these are the laymen, the mother and father of the family and the eldest son. To the women of the family, especially to the mother, falls the task of offering incense, wine, flowers, and other gifts to the family spirits. Each morning and each evening incense is lit for the following deities: the protecting deities placed in the center of the altar, who act as the liaison between the family and heaven's blessing; the ancestors housed in tablets to the west or *Yin* side of the altar; the miniature tiger placed on the ground directly under the center of the altar to guard against the entrance of the *Yin* spirits from the underworld into the family confines (the tiger spirit under the altar is subservient to the spirit of the soil, who performs a similar task by the graveside); the door gods (those separating the world of demonic spirits from the visible world of men) who protect the entrance of the house from the noxious influence of wandering *Yin* spirits (called *Sha* in mandarin and *Soat* in Taiwanese).

The Chinese household, therefore, and its ritual structure have a three-fold reference—to the plane of heavenly spirits above men, to the visible world in which man works and lives, and to the *Yin* world beneath the earth, where souls are punished in the afterlife. The twice-daily rituals in the family reflect the threefold cosmic stages, as does the division of the calendrical year into the three uneven periods ruled over by the spirits of heaven, earth, and the underworld. The three divisions of the spirits are worshipped in the daily household ritual, as well as in the calendrical cycle of annual customs and festivals.

Other functionaries called upon to assist in the ritual are the temple custodians, who read men's fortunes, the geomancers or *Feng-shui* experts, who find the most propitious place for a gravesite or a house through the means of the *Yin-Yang* five-element theory, and the medium or *Tang-ki*.

(The term *Tang-ki* is Amoy dialect for mandarin *T'ung-chi*, a "divining youth." Mediums are always referred to as *"T'ung"* or youthful, because they are supposed to be filled with spiritual power deriving from *Yang;* thus their state is like that of a new-born child, and so they are called "divining youths.") The medium is by definition a person who falls into a trance and becomes possessed of a demon.[20] During the possession he or she may be asked questions as to the state of an ancestor in hell, who may be untended and thus the source of sickness in the family, or any other question which the gods might be able to answer. Mediums are often controlled by the *Lü-shan* or Three Sisters sect Taoists. When in trance the mediums sometimes pierce their cheeks with long needles and cut their backs with swords or spiked balls, a proof of the efficacy of possession.

The highest functionary in the villages and cities of China where they are to be found practicing is the Taoist priest, who defines himself as the mandarin of the heavenly spirits.[21] The Taoists divide themselves into orders and ranks, with nine grades of excellence in each order. The nine grades are similar to those of the visible imperial mandarinate; the rank of a Taoist, however, is determined by the number of spirits he can summon, and the rituals which he knows how to perform. To the devout believers in the Chinese religion, the role of the Taoist is a despised and lowly one until his moment of triumph when he is called upon to exercise his marvelous powers as a mandarin of the gods. His is the power to summon and command the deities of the three stages, heaven, earth, and the underworld, and, at the *Chiao* festival of community renewal, to summon the heavenly *Yang* spirits to overcome the baleful forces of *Yin* and the demons of the underworld.

If *Yang* and *Yin* are principles which permeate the cosmos and which are basic both to the Chinese religion and to Taoism, it must be demonstrated how the principles act as an organizing force in shaping the structure of religion. The festivals of the Chinese calendrical year will be examined for evidence of the *Yin-Yang* five-element theory in the annual cycle of feasts and customs. The sources used in assembling the data are the *Taiwan Provincial Gazette*, the section on religions,[22] a popular manual sold in temple bookshops called *The Origin of the Spirits and the Annual Festivals* (of Taiwan) by *Cheng Sheng-ch'ang*,[23] and personal fieldnotes taken from storytellers in the temples of Taiwan.

In accounts of the annual festivals and customs of the Chinese religion as practiced on Taiwan, the following themes are consistently mentioned:

1.  Acts of goodness and virtue are associated with heaven, *Yang*, merit, and blessing, while evil and sinful acts, which deserve punishment from the gods, derive from *Yin*, the underworld of demons, and noxious spirits.

2.   The popular spirits of the Chinese religion are invariably seen to be virtuous men and women who died in some strange way, who spent their lives doing works in the public interest, and who were offered a localized cult of some sort after death, in order to channel their power for affecting the world of man.

3.   Demons are men or women who died a violent death, or who committed suicide, or who were maimed in such a fashion that they seek revenge on the world of men for their unfortunate positions in hell.

4.   Orphan souls who have no ancestor tablet or no offspring to control their localization and worship can be deified and made into helpful spirits by the process described in number two above.

A description of the festivals may best begin with the lunar New Year rites. It must be remembered, however, that the New Year is not celebrated on a single day, but is rather a series of events that signal the annual rebirth of *Yang* in the universe. The lunar New Year is preceded by the solar New Year, celebrated at the winter solstice festival, in the eleventh lunar month. The actual celebration of the lunar New Year begins on the twenty-fourth day of the twelfth lunar month, when the household gods are sent off to report to the Jade Emperor on the good and bad deeds of the household members during the past year. After the household spirits have left, the entire residence is given a complete scrubbing and cleaning, in preparation for the arrival of the heavenly spirits on the eve of the New Year. The cleansing symbolizes renewal, blessing, and purification from the powers of *Yin* and death, expelled at the end of the old year.[24]

## I.   First Lunar Month. Beginning of Spring. Element Wood

### *1.  First Month, First Day. The Celebration of the Lunar New Year*

The lunar New Year begins on the eve of the first day of the New Year, with the following list of rituals which last through the night into the first morning of the New Year. Each family decides for itself at exactly what moment the heavenly spirits arrive and thus initiate the blessing and renewal of the family for the coming year.

A.  Prescribed Rites

i.   The pasting of fortuitous verse in gold characters written on red paper over the doorposts and lintels of the main entrance. Many families specify the end sought by pasting over the door five red and gold talismans, welcoming the five primordial elements and the spirits that come with them.

ii.   Determining the moment of arrival of the heavenly gods, and the laying out of a banquet in their honor.[25] The sacrificial objects for the heavenly gods include sweet oranges, sweet rice cakes, cake, incense, wine, and new light (candles). The words for heaven (*T'ien*) and sweet (*t'ien*) are homonyms.

iii.    Banquet of cooked food for the ancestors; the end of the banquet, that is, the moment when the ancestors have eaten their fill, is determined by casting the wooden fortune blocks. When the *Yin* and the *Yang* side of two moon-shaped fortune blocks have fallen in balanced form together a number of times (symbolizing *Yin* and *Yang* in harmony), the food is taken away and reheated for the living members of the family.

iv.    The offering of a banquet of uncooked food for the spirits of the foundation, that is, the owners of the land who may have been there before the present occupants. These spirits are worshipped between the kitchen and the main hall, that is, they are not members of the family; children who have died young, the unmarried, and orphan spirits are worshipped in the same place. Small, silver-coated mock money is burned for them, whereas large, gold-coated mock money is burned for the heaven spirits. Gold is *Yang*, and silver is *Yin*.

v.    Banquet for the living members of the family assembled for the New Year's celebration. Women wear red flowers in their hair, and pleasant language must be spoken around the table. A small stove with coals from a newly lit fire is put under the table in the very center, symbolizing new life, new *Yang*, and unity of the entire family at the New Year.

vi.    The opening of the front door signals the arrival of the New Year and its blessings. Firecrackers are lit to scare away the evil *Yin* spirits. Paper money is burnt to the gods in order to win merit and blessings. Fortuitous greetings are exchanged between all members of the family. Children receive a red envelope with money in it from visiting members of the family.

vii.    All members of the family must bathe and put on new clothes. Early in the morning of the first day, the family goes to the temple to pray for blessing, then to the homes of male relatives and close friends to exchange New Year's greetings and presents. Five kinds of sweet candies, representing the blessing sought from the five elements newly come down from the heavens, are presented to all visitors.

B.    Taboo Acts from New Year's Eve until the Third Day of the New Year

i.    Walking out the door backwards (as when heavy things are carried out of doors), thus reversing the arrival of good luck and blessing.

ii.    Wasteful use of water, thus causing the forces of *Yin*, rain, and pestilent spirits to be prevalent in the coming year.

iii.    Physical work, such as the pounding of metals or any violent activity which might cause the heavenly spirits to leave, and the blessing of *Yang* to flow away.

iv. Tears, scolding, cursing, or angry words which might counteract the presence of the heavenly spirits. Man's acts must reflect the blessings desired for the coming year.

**2. *First Month, Fourth Day. Seeing off the Heavenly Spirits and Welcoming Back the Earth Spirits***

The heavenly spirits are sent back to their abodes in the "Prior Heavens," and the earth spirits, who monitor the good and bad acts of men, are brought back on the fourth day of the first month. The work activities of everyday life begin again.

**3. *First Month, Fifth Day. Visit by the Wife and Her Children to the Maternal Relatives of the Family***

**4. *First Month, Sixth Day. Birthday of the Monk Ch'ing-shui Tsu-shih***

*Ch'ing-shui Tsu-Shih* was a monk named *Ch'en Ying* who lived during the T'ang dynasty. He was born in Fukien province, Ch'üanchou prefecture, Anhsi district, the village of Hsiao-ku. After taking the vows of a Buddhist monk, he decided to leave the monastery and devote his life to austerities while working for the public good of the community. Worn out from repairing bridges, dikes, and roads, as well as helping the poor, he died at an early age. A popular cult soon developed. Shrines were built in his honor, and the people from Anhsi in Ch'üanchou still consider him their special spirit patron.[26] (Virtuous life, spent in working for the common good, untimely death, and popular devotion make a spirit-patron in the Chinese religion.)

**5. *First Month, Ninth Day. Birthday of the Jade Emperor***

The Jade Emperor, or *T'ien Kung,* Lord of Heaven, rules as the supreme deity of the spirits of the three stages of the visible world, heaven, earth, and underworld. He is to be distinguished from the Three Pure Ones, the highest trinity of the Taoist pantheon, whose feast day is properly celebrated on New Year's Day. During the village festival of renewal called *Chiao,* the Three Pure Ones are given a different spatial location in the north wall of the temple, with the Jade Emperor immediately beneath them to the left. On this day, the ninth of the first month, the male members of the family offer a special ritual to the Jade Emperor by raising a table up on stilted legs and offering five meats in his honor. The Jade Emperor is thought to be specially efficacious in granting boy babies. Women are not allowed to take part in his worship, to enter the room during prayers in his honor, or even to hang washing in the yard during his festival.

*6.  First Month, Thirteenth Day. Festival of Kuan Yü, the God of War*

*Kuan Yü* or *Kuan Kung* was a famous general of the Three Kingdoms period, at the end of the Han and prior to the founding of the Wei kingdom, ca. 220 A.D. He was a sworn brother and loyal servant of the pretender to the Han throne, *Liu Pei*. Due to his immense sense of loyalty, he is approved of by the official state religion as a patron of scholars. Since he was the first known spirit to keep accurate records of finances, he is also considered to be a patron spirit of bookkeepers and merchants. *Kuan Yü* died a violent death at the hands of his enemies and appears as a popular god in most temples, readily identifiable by his bright red face, black beard, ferocious countenance, and armor.

*7.  First Month, Fifteenth Day. Festival of the First of the Three Stages, the Spirits of Heaven. Festival of Lanterns*

Chinese religion divides the year and its festivals into three unequal segments. The first, from the first month, fifteenth day, until the seventh month, fifteenth day, is governed by the spirits of the heavens, under the rule of *Tz'u-wei Ta-ti*, giver of blessings. The second, from the seventh month, fifteenth day, until the tenth month, fifteenth day, is governed by the spirits of earth, under the rule of *Ch'ing-hsü Ta-ti*, who forgives sins. The third, from the tenth month until the New Year, is governed by the spirits of the waters, under the rule of *Tung-yin Ta-ti*, the dispeller of evil spirits. The three stages of the macrocosm correspond to the three sections of the body in the microcosm, head, chest, and belly of man.

The rituals special to the first month, fifteenth day, include the presentation of lantern displays to the local temple, a banquet offered first to the heavenly gods in the temple, then brought home for the family to eat, and the presenting of toy lanterns to children to be carried around in the streets. The symbolic carrying of lanterns in order to identify spirits or guide spirits on their way, the movement of lanterns through the streets, the dragon dance performed in the evening of the fifteenth are all to be contrasted to the ceremonies performed on the night of the seventh month, fifteenth day, when lanterns are floated in the rivers and food is laid out for the hungry ghosts. The activities are also to be contrasted to those of the eighth month, fifteenth day, when rest and contemplating of the full moon are observed rather than movement and carrying of lanterns (representing new fire and *Yang*). The dragon dance done through the streets of Chinese villages and cities is to be interpreted in the eyes of the Taoist, the temple custodians, and the storyteller as symbolic of a search for the drop of pure *Yang* hidden in the sea of *Yin*. The dragon eternally chases after a bright red ball, carried by a boy at the head of the procession. When swallowed, the red ball produces longevity, immortality, and life with the spirits in the Prior Heavens. The significance of the lanterns, dragon dance, and festivities is related to *Yang*, immortality, and blessing.

## II.   The Second Lunar Month

### 1.   *Second Month, Second Day. Birthday of the Lord of the Soil*

The spirit of the soil, *T'u-ti Kung*, variously translated as Duke of the Soil, Lord of the Soil, Sire of the Soil, and so forth, is also called *Fu-te Cheng-shen*, "Orthodox Spirit Who Blesses Virtue"; he has a double role in Chinese religion. On the one hand, he stands by the side of the grave, keeping the spirits in the world of *Yin* separated from the visible world of man. On the other hand, he is enshrined in the village squares, wayside shrines, and households of China as the official who oversees the good and bad acts of the community performed in public. His is the role of the *Kung-ts'ao*, the liaison official who is appointed by the Jade Emperor to guard the local community, rewarding good and punishing evil. He is the earthly servant and mandarin of the Yellow Emperor, god of the center, and as such can cause the crops to flourish and the earth to yield blessing. Merchants worship him on the second and sixteenth of every month as the god who brings wealth and blessing. On the second day of the second month, the "first" day of the New Year on which he is worshipped, puppet shows and opera performances are sponsored by the temple committees in his honor. Turtle cakes, symbols of longevity, are laid in front of his shrines. The characters for wealth (*Lu*) and blessing (*Fu*) are inscribed on the turtle's back, thus symbolically representing the continuing reception of these gifts through the mediation of the Lord of the Soil.[27]

### 2.   *Second Month, Third Day. Festival of Wen Ch'ang, Patron of Scholars*

*Wen Ch'ang* is the name of a constellation composed of six stars in the northern heavens just beyond Ursa Major. The spirits residing in the constellation's six stars are said to be *Ta Chiang*, the great general; *Tz'u Chiang*, lieutenant general; *Kuei Chiang*, the noble general; *Ssu Lu*, the controller of wealth; *Ssu Ming*, the controller of life; and *Ssu Tsai*, the controller of natural calamity.[28] The six are gods also patronized by the Taoists, a fact which demonstrates the difference between the gods of the Prior Heavens, the unchanging world of pure *Yang* from whence the Taoist pantheon derives, and the Posterior Heavens of the Three Stages, from whence the pantheon of the Chinese religion is constructed. Many of the spirits belong to both systems; one of these is *Wen Ch'ang,* the patron of scholars.

In the popular religion the first of the six deities is called *Hsin T'ung;* the second is *K'uei Sheng,* the ugly *Chin-shih* literatus who passed highest in the imperial examinations. His features were so repulsive that the emperor refused to employ him, and *K'uei Sheng* committed suicide. From his position in the *Wen Ch'ang* constellation he is called upon to help poor scholars, and to exorcise evil demons, his features frightening not only emperors, but also harmful spirits. The third is Lord *Wen Heng;* the fourth is Lord Red Coat, *Chu-i;* the fifth is *Lü Tung-pin,* the scholar-Taoist who is also worshipped as one of the eight immortals, *Pa Hsien*; and the last is *Ssu Ming,* the keeper of the book of life and death.

### 3.   Second Month, Sixteenth Day. Birthday of Lao-tzu

i.   *Lao-tzu* or *Lao Chun* (Lord Lao) fulfills a threefold role in Chinese religion. He is the third of the Taoist trinity, the *Tao-te* Heavenly Worthy, lord of the Great Purity realm of the Prior Heavens. As such he is a part of the orthodox Taoist tradition. He is also a popular deity in the Chinese religion, whose festival is celebrated on the sixteenth day of the second month. Finally, he is patron of the heterodox *Lü Shan* sect of Taoists, whose devotees act as interpreters and masters of the mediums when possessed by a spirit in trance.

ii.   The festival of *Yüeh Fei,* the brave general of the Sung dynasty, is also celebrated on this day. At the early age of thirty-nine, *Yüeh Fei* was treacherously slain by a jealous friend. He is worshipped by the believers in Chinese popular religion as a powerful spirit, due to his unwavering loyalty in defending the Sung emperor, his unfortunate death, and the efficacy of prayers addressed to him as a spiritual mediator. A deep-fried bread sold in the streets every morning as a substantial part of the Taiwanese diet is called *"Yu-chia Kuei,"* "Oil-Fried Demon," in memory of the evil official who had *Yüeh Fei* slain. The frying of the long sticks of bread in the morning symbolizes punishment for the soul of the man who had his friend killed.

iii.   The festival of *K'ai Chang Sheng Wang,* the official who first colonized Changchou prefecture during the T'ang dynasty, is also cele-brated on this day. The majority of the Chinese immigrants to Taiwan came from Changchou and Ch'üanchou prefectures in southern Fukien province on the China mainland during the late Ming and Ch'ing periods. The people of Changchou pay special respect to *K'ai Chang Sheng Wang,* the "Holy Ruler Who Pioneered in Changchou." His name is said to have been *Ch'en Yüan-kuang,* the general in charge of the troops who settled and colonized

Changchou during the T'ang dynasty. Worn out with public service and good deeds, he died and was venerated by the people as a god.

**4.   *Second Month, Nineteenth Day. Birthday of Kuanyin Buddha.***

*Kuanyin*, the Chinese goddess of mercy, is the Indian Buddhist *Boddhisattva Avalokitesvara*. In the move from India to China, the *Boddhisattva* took on the attributes of a woman, and was adopted as a feminine deity in the Chinese religion. *Kuanyin* epitomizes the virtue of mercy, reaching down into hell to free the suffering, coming to the aid of the distressed, doing those deeds associated with the role of a woman. The Taoists invoke *Kuanyin Buddha* during the ritual performed after burial to free the soul from the ten bureaus of punishments in hell. The devout believers of the popular religion often hang a picture of *Kuanyin* over the family altar, or keep her statue with the household deities in the center of the family shrine. *Kuanyin*, therefore, appears as a powerful spirit to invoke in the continuing battle against the forces of *Yin* and evil.

**5.   *Second Month, Twenty-Second Day. Birthday of Kuo Hsing Wang***

*Kuo Hsing Wang* was a poor cowherd boy who died at the age of sixteen. He is especially worshipped by people from Ch'üanchou prefecture in Fukien province. A geomancer predicted that after his early death he would be given great spiritual power. A cult was soon set up in the boy's honor; he became a patron of geomancers, of curing by Chinese medicine, and of immigrants to Taiwan from Ch'üanchou county in Fukien. His other names are *Sheng Wang Kung*, Lord Holy King; *Pao-an Tsun-wang*, Worthy King Who Preserves Peace; and *Kuang-tse Tsun-wang*, Worthy King Kuang-tse.

## III.   The Third Lunar Month

**1.   *Third Month, Third Day. Birthday of Hsüan-t'ien Shang-ti***

i.   *Hsüan-t'ien Shang-ti*, Emperor of the Somber Heavens, is patron of the Pole Star Taoist sect, protector of the Ming dynasty, and tutelary spirit for butchers and barbers. His other names are *Shang-ti Tieh*, the Old Emperor; *Shang-ti Kung*, Lord Emperor; *Chen-wu Ta-ti*, Great Emperor Realized Warrior; and *Pei-chi Sheng-shen Chun*, Lord of the Spirits of the Pole Star. The names, in fact, reveal his role in the Chinese religion, and in Taoism. As patron of the militaristic Pole Star sect from Wutang Shan in Hupei province, he is a spirit efficacious in exorcisms and in the suppressing of the evil demons subordinate to *Yin*.

Under the feet of the statues carved in his memory are always to be found a turtle and a serpent. The serpent represents *Jen* or *Yang* water, and the tortoise symbolizes *Kuei* or *Yin* water. When the *Yin* and the *Yang* aspects of the element water are joined under the feet of the deity of the north Pole Star, there is life, birth, and blessing. When the *Yang* and the *Yin* aspects of the element water are separated, there is death, wilting, and misfortune. The god of the north Pole Star *Hsüan-t'ien Shang-ti* thus appears as the euhemerization of the spirit of water, and as arbiter of life and death, blessing and calamity.

*Hsüan-t'ien Shang-ti*, according to a legend popular in Taiwan, was a butcher who owned a magical knife. Whatever the knife touched was instantly cut in two. *Hsüan-t'ien Shang-ti* feared that if his knife fell into the wrong hands, it could be an instrument that would cause harm to men rather than help them. He, therefore, plunged the knife into his belly and jumped into a river, thus protecting mankind from the dangerous weapon. His belly became the turtle and his intestines the serpent on which he stands.[29] Southern and central Taiwan are especially devoted to his worship, and the cult is popular in Chia-i city from which most of Taiwan's barbers originate.

ii.    *The Cold Food* festival is celebrated shortly after the festival of the third month, third day, and prior to the *Ch'ing Ming* festival, 105 days after the winter solstice. The feast day is dedicated to the memory of *Chieh-tzu T'ui*, a minister of the kingdom of Chin during the Warring States period. *Chieh-tzu T'ui* refused to serve the corrupt king of Chin. Taking his parents, he fled into a deep forest. So poor was their life that he was forced to cut the flesh from his legs in order to feed his parents. The king of Chin sent his messengers to burn down the forest and thus force *Chieh-tzu T'ui* to come out and resume office. But *Chieh* chose to remain inside the holocaust, and burned to death. For this reason he was honored as a deity, and to this day cooked food is not eaten on his festival in memory of his tragic death.[30]

iii.    *The Ch'ing Ming* festival. The *Ch'ing Ming* or "Clear Brightness" festival is celebrated 105 days after the winter solstice and is the day for cleaning and repairing graves. A grave is symbolically covered with a new set of tile roofing, by pressing sheets of yellow paper into the soil that covers the coffin. A special ritual is offered to the Lord of the Soil, who stands guard by the side of the grave. His role of protecting the world of men from the spirits of *Yin* and evil is reinforced by the *Ch'ing Ming* festival. Since all the members of the family walk from their homes to the hillsides outside the towns and villages, *Ch'ing Ming* is traditionally a day when boys and girls of good families may see each other and press for marriage arrangements with their respective parents. In many parts of China the cold-food festival is also observed on this day.

## 2.    *Third Month, Fifteenth Day. Birthday of Pao-sheng Ta-ti*

*Pao-sheng Ta-ti*, the Great Emperor Who Protects Life, is considered by the Taiwanese to be the patron deity of Chinese medicine. He was born in Fukien province, Ch'üanchou prefecture, Tung-an district, during the Sung dynasty. Because he led a very virtuous life, a spirit appeared to him by the seashore and revealed a set of talismanic secrets and Chinese medicines for curing illness. Worn out by a life spent in helping his fellowmen, he died at the age of fifty-eight, and was immediately given veneration as a powerful deity by the local populace.

## 3.    *Third , Twenty-Third Day. Birthday of Matsu*

*Matsu*, the virgin goddess who is patron of fishermen and farmers, is one of the most popular deities on Taiwan. Reputed to be a fisherman's daughter named *Lin Muo*, she was born on Michou island, southern Fukien, during the Sung dynasty. As a child she was very pious, given to long periods of meditation and silence. One day, while washing clothes by a well, a spirit appeared to her in a vision, and revealed a series of talismans for expelling evil and helping men. At the age of twenty-one she died, unmarried, and was almost immediately given public veneration. Various emperors have granted *Matsu* royal titles, including "Heavenly Empress" awarded by the K'ang Hsi emperor during the Ch'ing dynasty, and "Holy Mother of the Heavens Above" given by a later Ch'ing emperor, *Ch'ien Lung*. Two frightful demons, "See a Thousand Miles" and "Follow the Wind Ears," whom she quelled by her magic talismans, appear as servants by her side in popular temple settings. The two deities act as servants, reporting on the needs of devout believers, so that *Matsu* may rush to their aid.

## 4.    *Third Month, Twenty-Sixth Day. Birthday of Chang Tao-ling*

*Chang Tao-ling* is the spiritual patron and founder of Heavenly Master sect *Cheng-i* (Orthodox One) Taoism. He was born, according to legend, in Kiangsi province, southeast China, and traveled to the western province of Szechuan ca. 140 A.D. to found the Five Bushels of Rice, or the Heavenly Master sect Taoist movement. *Lao-tzu* was supposed to have appeared to him in a vision atop a mountain, where the method of curing illness through letters addressed to the Spirits of the Three Realms was developed. One letter was addressed to the heavenly bureau of spirits and burned on a mountain top. A second letter was addressed to the earthly bureau and buried in the ground. A third document was addressed to the water spirits and thrown in a river. The addressing of official documents to the three realms, though changed somewhat through the ages, is still practiced in the Taoist rituals of today. Tradition says that *Chang Tao-ling* and his wife were both "wafted up to the heavens in broad daylight" to the accompaniment of heavenly music and chariots filled with spirits. The figure of *Chang Tao-ling* is to be seen in many Taiwanese temples, astride a fearsome tiger, symbolizing that the magic of the Heavenly Master sect can subdue the tiger, the mythical animal which represents *Yin*.[31]

## IV.  The Fourth Lunar Month. Beginning of Summer. Element Fire and Color Red Dominate

### 1.  *The Fourth Month, Fourth Day. Birthday of the Buddha*

*Buddha's* birthday is celebrated with great honor in Buddhist monasteries as well as in the temples of the Chinese popular religion. *Buddha*, like all the other spirits in the Chinese religious system, lived a life of great merit. Prayers addressed to him are efficaciously answered. The rituals performed in his honor are repeated in local temples by teams of Buddhist priests and nuns. Other Buddhist figures such as *Kuanyin*, the goddess of mercy, and *Ti-tsang Wang*, the god who frees souls from hell, were of obvious Buddhist origin but long ago identified in the minds of the people as powerful spirits in the Chinese religious system. The Taoists wear the crown of *Ti-tsang Wang* when performing the *P'u-tu* ritual for releasing the souls and impersonate *Kuanyin Buddha* when leading the soul of the departed through the ten stages of hell.

### 2.  *Fourth Month, Fourteenth Day. Birthday of Lü Tung-pin*

*Lü Tung-pin*, the scholar among the eight immortals, goes by many titles. He is called *Ts'un Yang-tzu*, Pure *Yang* Child; *Fu-yu Ti-chun*, Lord Emperor Who Brings Aid; and *Lü Tsu-shih*, Lord Ancestor *Lü*. Though the history of the real person named *Lü Tung-pin* is difficult to establish, he is said to have been a man of the T'ang period, who was a devout Taoist. He made a pilgrimage to the five sacred peaks and was trained as a Taoist at the monastic center on Lu Shan in Kiangsi, the home of the heterodox Three Sisters sect. The orthodoxy of *Lü Tung-pin* is not questioned, however; having attained the *Chin-shih*, or doctor of letters, and a high rank in the imperial mandarinate, he was warned in a vision that he should leave public life and spend the rest of his years in the quest for immortality. He did so, and like many of the spirits in the popular religion was "wafted up to the heavens" as an immortal in broad daylight.

### 3.  *Fourth Month, Twenty-Sixth Day. Birthday of Shen Nung, Spirit of Summer*

i.  *Shen Nung*, whose other name is *Yen Ti*, is god of summer, patron of agriculture and pottery, and inventor of Chinese medicine. He is one of the five spirits of the Taoist pantheon called upon to restore the pristine order of the universe. He rules over the south, the primordial vapor of summer, red, and the element fire. Statues of him in the local temples show a round-bellied, wide-eyed god with a leaf skirt and a branch of freshly harvested millet in his hand.

ii.    Birthday of the gods of pestilence, *Wang Yeh;* summer with its blessings of good crops and plenty also brings an increase in summer colds and disease. The gods of pestilence, the *Wang Yeh* or "Old Kings," are found with the Chinese and with coastal peoples throughout southeast Asia and are closely related to the *Wu-t'ung* spirits of the China mainland, who have similar qualities. The sea-coast peoples put the gods of pestilence in a boat, and push them out to sea; when the boat drifts ashore, a new shrine is set up in their honor. Every three years or so the rite must be repeated in villages which worship the gods, thus proliferating worship of the evil spirits along the sea coast. *Wang Yeh* is a general classification for public officials who commit suicide and are afterwards worshipped as fearful spirits by the local populace.

## V.    The Fifth Lunar Month

### 1.    *Fifth Month, Fifth Day. Festival Initiating the Summer Solstice*

This day is called *Tuan Wu Chieh,* the beginning of the "noon" in the annual cycle of festivities. *Yang* is soon to reach zenith and *Yin* to be reborn in the cosmos as predominant principle, bringing about the maturation of crops, harvest, winter, and death. The day's festivities include the famous dragon boat race, which draws many spectators, and is variously interpreted as a fertility rite, a rite for rain, originally a human sacrifice to the river dragon, and a commemorative act for men or women who have drowned in the river. The famous poet *Ch'ü Yüan,* who committed suicide by jumping into the Milo river in Hunan, is commemorated on this day by throwing glutinous rice cakes into the water.

All the devout believers in the popular religion are advised to bathe in sulfur water on this day as a means of protection against illness. Charms representing the five venomous creatures, centipede, scorpion, snake, lizard, and toad, are hung as necklaces around children's necks to protect them from summer colds. The Taoists most frequently expel the demons of pestilence during this period by pushing them out to sea in a boat. Thus water-oriented rites at the beginning of the summer heat curb the forces which cause sickness and seek to control the source from which *Yin* is reborn.

## VI.   The Sixth Lunar Month

There are no significant festivals during the sixth month. On the sixth day of the sixth month bedding and clothes are traditionally put out in the sun to air and to kill the dampness and mold which begin in the early months of summer. The farming season is at its height, and thus the Chinese religion leaves the farmers free to accomplish their many tasks. Marriages are frowned upon in the sixth month. American divorces are many, says a Taiwanese proverb, because a sixth-month marriage is only half a marriage.

## VII.   The Seventh Lunar Month. Beginning of Autumn. Element Metal and Vapor White

### 1.   *Seventh Month, Seventh Day. Opening of the Gates of Hell*

On the first day of the seventh month, the first day of the season of autumn, the Gates of Hell are thought to be opened and the imprisoned souls are freed. The hungry orphan souls with no offspring are thought to wander about, looking for sustenance in the visible world. The merit of a food offering wins release for the suffering souls and blessing for the giver.

The Chinese religion is explicit about the punishments meted out to the souls in hell. Scenes on temple walls and illustrations in popular pamphlets illustrate the various punishments in graphic detail. An unjust money lender is eternally run over by a Taipei taxi; thieves and murderers are pounded on a heated anvil; women who die in childbirth are plunged into a pool of blood. The seventh month is the time to free the tortured from their punishments. The opening of the Gates of Hell signals the beginning of the *P'u-tu* festival for granting a general amnesty to the souls in hell by a community banquet. The *P'u-tu* was formerly rotated from village to village in parts of Taiwan so that there were continuing festivities from the first until the fifteenth day of the seventh month. In present-day Taiwan the government has restricted the *P'u-tu* festival to the fifteenth day only.

### 2.   *Seventh Month, Seventh Day. Festival of the Seven Young Ladies*

The Seven Young Ladies are believed to protect children until the age of sixteen, and the festival of puberty. On this day young girls try to thread a needle by moonlight, an accomplishment efficacious for marrying a good husband. Powder and cosmetics are offered as a sacrifice to the youngest of the seven maids, the weaving girl. Due to the bliss of marital relations with the cowherd boy, she neglected her task of weaving, and so was punished by the Jade Emperor; she and her lover were separated eternally by the Milky Way, and are allowed together only on this one night a year.

### 3.   Seventh Month, Fifteenth Day. Festival of the Earth Spirits

The seventh month, fifteenth day, is the beginning of the rule of the earth spirits, the second of the three stages of the world of spirits. On this day the most important ritual is the feeding of the hungry orphan souls who have been released from the fiery underworld, and since the first day of the seventh month have been wandering about the world of men. The *Ch'eng Huang* deity, chief mandarin of the city's gods and judge of punishments in the underworld after death, is brought out in a palanquin to survey the city on this day. A procession of all the deities in the *Ch'eng Huang* temple precedes the *Ch'eng Huang* deity's palanquin in order to arrest all unruly demons. In the evening a *P'u-tu* banquet is laid out by each family to feed the hungry souls before sending them off on their journey to the heavens. Finally, each family joins a procession to the sea, or to the nearest river, to float a lantern to guide the souls on their return journey.

### 4.   Seventh Month, Thirtieth Day. Closing of the Gates of Hell

Tradition says that all of the souls freed on the first day of the seventh month must return by the thirtieth day (or the twenty-ninth if the lunar month has only twenty-nine days) or be condemned to wander eternally as lost souls. Such spirits are called *Keng* spirits, that is, spirits without a place in the cosmos to which they can return. Each family lays a repast by the doorstep, wrapped for a traveler, in order to speed the souls on their way.

## VIII.   The Eighth Lunar Month

### 1.   Eighth Month, Third Day. Birthday of the God of the Hearth

The god of the hearth, *Tsao Chun,* is also called *Ssu-ming Tsao Chun,* Controller of Life, Lord of the Stove, and *Hu-t'a T'ien Tsun,* Heavenly Worthy Who Protects the House. *Tsao Chun* is the keeper of the records of man's good and evil deeds. He reports annually to the Jade Emperor on the twenty-fourth day of the twelfth lunar month. Evil deeds stemming from the principle of *Yin* are recorded in the book of death for punishment in hell, while good deeds are recorded in the book of life for reward both in the present world and in the hereafter.

The god of the hearth is said to have been the son of a wealthy man who lived at the beginning of the Chou empire, ca. 1050 B.C. After his father's death, he wasted the family's substance, and finally had to sell his wife into slavery in order to survive. One day, reduced to starvation, he went begging and came by chance to the house where his wife worked. Stunned by his poor condition, the wife allowed him into her master's kitchen, to eat his fill. Unexpectedly the master of the house came into the kitchen. *Tsao Chun* hid in the chimney. The master of the house ordered a fire lit and water boiled for his bath. *Tsao Chun* was thus burned to death and subsequently appointed by the Heavenly Emperor as guardian of the hearth. From his position near the family stove, he always eats his fill, and reports on the good and bad deeds of the family members from the best vantage point, where women congregate and talk.

*2.   Eighth Month, Fifteenth Day. Festival of the Autumn Moon*

The festival of the eighth month, fifteenth day, is concerned with stillness and composure, the reverse of the first month, fifteenth day, which was a festival of extreme motion and agitation. The moon, the symbol for *Yin*, is thought to contain within its depths the secret of longevity, just as the bright pearl hidden in the depths of the ocean is the drop of *Yang* from which nature is annually reborn. Activities which bring heaven's blessing on this evening are: gazing at the moon's reflection in water, composing of poetry, walking in the cool evening while watching the full moon. Moon-shaped sweet cakes are sold in all the stores and given to relatives and friends. Local opera troupes and puppet shows perform in the temple plazas, sponsored by the wealthy of the community or by those fulfilling a vow to a god.

The festival also commemorates the goddess of the moon, *Ch'ang-o* the wife of *Hou-hsi*, the man credited with shooting down the nine unruly suns, cause of drought and famine. For his reward the Queen Mother of the Western Heavens gave him the pill of immortality. But his wife stole the pill and swallowed it. She was immediately changed to an immortal, but punished eternally by being imprisoned in the cold palace of the moon.

# IX.   The Ninth Lunar Month

*1.   Ninth Month, Ninth Day. Birthday of T'ai-tzu Yeh*

*T'ai-tzu Yeh*, the naughty child god, is also called *Na-ch'o*, and "Primordial Master of the Central *T'an*-Altar," a Taoist title. Legend says that he was a child born with miraculous spiritual powers. At seven years of age, he killed the son of the dragon king of the eastern ocean. A series of battles followed, in which *T'ai-tzu Yeh* bullied both men and gods until his teacher *T'ai-i* managed to subdue him. For his punishment *T'ai-tzu Yeh* was told to commit suicide by disembowelment. The cult of *T'ai-tzu Yeh* is semi-official and semi-heterodox. He is a spirit invoked by the *Lü Shan* Three Sisters sect Taoists, and is a favorite patron of the demonic possession rites performed by the mediums or *Tang-ki* of Taiwan. He is seen in temple paintings as a terrifying god riding a magic wheel and carrying a thunderbolt.

## 2.  Ninth Month, Twenty-Eighth Day. Birthday of Confucius

*Confucius*, object of the state-approved cult of scholars, is also a spirit popular in the Chinese religion of the common people. The government sponsors a feather dance performed by young men in front of his temple. To the people *Confucius* ranks with *Kuan Yü, Wen Ch'ang,* and other state-approved deities as a god of scholars.

## X.  The Tenth Lunar Month. Beginning of Winter. Element Water and Seasonal Color Black

### 1.  Tenth Month, Tenth Day. Festival of Yü the Great

*Yü* the Great was the demiurge who controlled the flood waters and divided ancient China into nine provinces, after the model of the *Lo Shu,* the "magic square" which was discovered in the Lo River. When he was appointed by the Emperor Shun to stop the raging waters, a spirit appeared to *Yü* by the Yellow River and gave him a magic symbol called the *Ho-t'u,* the chart of the Yellow River. The chart, according to legend, was the *Ling-pao* Five Talismans, the secret writs and ritual which the Taoists still use to effect community renewal. The five talismans were magic formulae for controlling all the spirits of the three stages; by using them *Yü* was able to cause the five primordial elements and their euhemerized spirits to restore nature to its pristine state of order, life, and blessing. When *Yü* had used the talismans to stop the floods, he buried them atop Mao Shan, a sacred mountain near Nanjing.[32]

The day also commemorates all of the famous men who died by drowning; the list is a long one, and includes *Chi'ü Yüan* and *Li Po,* great poets from the past.

### 2.  Tenth Month, Fifteenth Day. Beginning of the Rule of the Water Spirits

The fifteenth day of the tenth month is the beginning of the rule of the spirits from the third stage of the world, the water and the underworld deities. The day is centered around temple rituals. Both Buddhist and Taoist temples sponsor the same program, which is in effect a one-day *Chiao* ritual of renewal. The central rite of the day, as on the fifteenth of the seventh month, is the offering of a *P'u-tu* banquet to free the souls in the watery regions of the underworld. The tenth month is otherwise not a month of festivals, since the farmers are busy with the second harvest and preparation for a winter planting.

## XI.   The Eleventh Lunar Month

### 1.   *The Winter Solstice. The Solar New Year*

The winter solstice usually falls during the eleventh month of the lunar calendar. The ritual consists of burning paper money and offering a banquet for ancestors, following which rice balls are pasted around the house in the five sources of blessing, that is, the door, the main room, the kitchen, the well, and the bedroom. Sometimes the rice balls are put in the toilet and animal pens. A sweet soup made of smaller rice balls colored red and white is given to guests and served at the evening banquet. In many families the dinner table is placed against the family altar, symbolizing that the ancestors are the guests of honor.

The great *Chiao* festival of renewal is celebrated during the eleventh and the twelfth months.[33] There are no other significant festivals during this time, since the *Chiao* truly involves the strength and attention of the entire community.

## XII.   The Twelfth Lunar Month

### 1.   *Twelfth Month, Sixteenth Day. Last Festival of the Soil God*

*T'u-ti Kung*, the tutelary deity of the soil, is worshipped on the second and the sixteenth day of every month, starting from the second day of the second month and ending on the sixteenth day of the twelfth month, before the lunar New Year festivities. The year's accounts are calculated and employees hired or released for the coming year. A banquet must be given by employers for employees, and a bonus given to help defray family expenses for the New Year. The lord of the soil is especially worshipped as patron of businesses on this day.

### 2.   *Twelfth Month, Twenty-Fourth Day. Seeing Off the Household Spirits*

On the twenty-fourth day of the twelfth month, the household spirits are "sent off to the heavens" in a rite symbolizing the purification of the house for the coming of the heavenly spirits on New Year's eve. The house is scrubbed and cleaned thoroughly. The end of the old year, Yin, and the uncleanliness are thus expelled by the day's activities; Yang, the New Year, and heavenly spirits are the theme of the approaching New Year. The ceremonies of the great Chiao festival of renewal will be seen to parallel the festivities preceding the celebration of the lunar New Year.

The festivals, rituals, and hagiographies of the gods described above are particular to Taiwan, a small fraction of the total physical and cultural heritage of China. The rituals and festivals differ not only for each province and district of China, but even among the cities and villages of Taiwan. The hypothesis that the Yin-Yang five-element theory acts as an organizing principle throughout the totality of Chinese religion is perhaps the only possible interpretation that unites the variegated festivals and customs of China. Throughout China, or wherever Chinese religion is practiced, the year and its festivals can be divided into two great sections, the first dominated by the principle *Yang*, growth, and blessing, the other ruled by the principle *Yin*, harvest, and rest. The spirits, following the festivals of the year, are divided into three unequal segments: the heavenly spirits rule over that part of the year dominated by Yang; the earth spirits and the water spirits rule over the second part of the year regulated by *Yin*. The four seasons and the five elements are personified by spirits who bear the blessing or the particular character of the season.

Thus the birth of *Yang* at the winter solstice is celebrated by the arrival of the heavenly spirits. The birth of *Yin* at the summer solstice is accompanied by rituals directed to the water, to the expulsion of the demons of pestilence, and to the freeing of souls in the underworld. Blessing is associated with the spirits of the heavens, and calamity with the spirits of the underworld.

The popular spirits of the Chinese religion whose hagiographies appear in the above pages appear to have been men and women who died a strange death by violence, suicide, or strenuous effort for the common good. Had they not been deified by popular devotion, they would have fulfilled the definition of an orphan soul or a wandering spirit, that is, no ancestors to burn incense, no localization of cult, and transformation into a demon. Acts of merit, virtuous deeds for the common good, and strenuous activity are all derivatives of the principle *Yang*, which brings blessing. Acts which harm men, antisocial behavior, and violence derive from the principle *Yin* and are to be punished. Normalcy is associated with the regular progress of man from childhood (*Yang*) through adulthood to old age and death (*Yin*). Deviation from the pattern of nature creates a spirit (overbalance of *Yang*) or a demon (overbalance of *Yin*). The basic operational principle of the popular religion is to promote acts stemming from *Yang*, thus winning blessing, and to suppress deeds stemming from *Yin*, thus averting calamity. The genius of the Chinese religious mind is to substitute the abstract philosophical principle for a personified deity, and thus the gods and demons of the pantheon of the Chinese cosmos represent an euhemerization of the *Yin-Yang* five-element theory.

Taoism not only confirms for the popular religion the *Yin-Yang* five element theory, but is itself firmly based on the same cosmic principles. The rites of orthodox religious Taoism derive from the *Yin-Yang* five-element school, from the rituals of feudal China, and from various movements in popular Chinese religion originating in the Han dynasty and shortly thereafter. The influence of Buddhism on Taoism is unmistakable and can be seen in the desire for universal salvation and in various rituals which are shared in common. But the theological and cosmological principles on which Taoism is based are unmistakably Chinese, and are not substantially different from the foundations of Chinese religion. On the popular village level, Taoist priest, village temple, and ritual are so closely united as to be practically identical; where he lives and operates, the Taoist is in fact the priest of the Chinese religion.

The influence of Taoism on Chinese religion is functional; a Taoist is called on to perform certain of the rites of passage. Rites which ease childbirth, cure sickness, and exorcise evil are his specialty. Temple rituals on the birthday of a god or on a major festival occasion are his prerogative. The burial of the dead and the accompanying of the soul through the ten stages of hell are his special duty and obligation. The one occasion, on which the powers of the Taoist to organize and inform the popular religion are most evident, is during the celebration of the great ritual of renewal called *Chiao*. In this festival the Taoist is called upon to perform the liturgy of orthodox Heavenly Master sect Taoism, to illuminate the organizing force of Chinese religion through the community festival of renewal.

# II

# The Chiao Festival:
# An Etic Description

The village festival called *Chiao* is the pinnacle of the celebrations of Chinese religion. It is performed once every cycle of sixty years, or as close to that time as the village and the tutelary gods of the local temple agree.[1] Preparations for the festival take years, and the village temple is repaired at great expense. The village elders and leaders are called upon to support the event, both politically and economically. A committee, directly responsible for the immediate preparations, is selected by casting fortune blocks before the main shrine in the temple.

Each clan and each of the more influential families within the clans are expected to donate generously to the temple repairs and to the immediate decorations. Participating families must each sponsor a votive lamp called *Tou* within the temple. The lamps vary in number from a minimal 150 for a smaller, three-day *Chiao* festival to as many as 240 or 360 for a five- or nine-day *Chiao* celebration. The votive lamps are ornate wooden containers, usually hand-carved, and filled with pure white rice. Into the rice are inserted a sword, a scales, a ruler, scissors, and a mirror.[2] In the very center of the "bushel" or *Tou* is laid an oil lamp with a long wick. The name of the family and the deity in whose honor the lamp is given appear on the outside of the container. The placing of the bushel and the importance of the deity honored by its contribution in the temple are directly related to the affluence and importance of the contributing family, that is, to the amount of money given for the celebration.

For a month before the festival is to begin, villagers are expected to purify themselves by acts of repentance and to rectify past misdemeanors. Acts of penitence such as abstaining from meat and the giving of alms are encouraged. Articles of clothing associated with death, such as wool, leather, and the color white, are avoided.[3] On the last day before the ritual festivities begin, all are expected to bathe, as a sort of ritual purification.

The village temple, the focal point of political, economic, and recreational life of the community, is given special attention. With the reconstruction and decorations completed, the temple must be specially prepared for the elite secret rituals to be performed within its precincts. A number of men are appointed to guard the entrances. All but one of the doors of the temple are sealed, and no one wearing wool, leather, or white-colored garments is allowed to enter the temple. The gods of the folk religion, called *Shen-ming* or "Bright Spirits" in technical terms, are removed from their places of honor along the north wall of the temple and put in the south by the entrance, from which place the people usually worship.[4] All this activity is in preparation for the bringing of the Heavenly Worthies, the special object of the Taoist ritual worship, into the sacred temple area.

## The Invited Guests

Three classes of guests, mortal and immortal, are invited to be present at the festival. First, various deities from famous shrines around Taiwan are invited. The more popular deities of the Chinese religion, such as the Jade Emperor, *Kuanyin,* the Buddhist goddess of mercy, *Matsu,* the virgin patron of fishermen and farmers, *Kuan-yü,* the god of war, and *Chang T'ien-shih,* the founder of Heavenly Master sect Taoism, are given especially prepared structures called *T'an* as temporary lodging.[5] Each of the wealthier families of the community sponsors a *T'an* in the visiting deities' honor. The more *T'an* constructed, the greater the merit and praise for the *Chiao* festival in the eyes of the surrounding villages, and the more abundant are the blessings won from the gods. The family which sponsors a *T'an* provides on each day of the festival a new set of silk clothing for the effigy of the deity housed there. The *T'an* are sometimes three or four stories in height, and become museums to house the family's artifacts and to entertain visiting mortals as well as spirits. The lesser deities invited, small, wooden statues from neighborhood shrines and temples, are housed on a platform in front of the temple.

Second, human visitors are invited to attend the festival. Guests come from all over Taiwan to witness the event. Close relatives, friends, and even foreign acquaintances are asked to be present for the great banquet on the last day. The *Chiao* is a communal festival, uniting the village and its clans with neighboring villages, and winning merit for all of the living, as well as a general amnesty for all of the souls in the underworld.

Finally, the ancestors and the souls in the underworld are invited. The final day of the *Chiao* festival provides three banquets, one for the heavenly spirits, one for the suffering souls in the underworld, and one for the living.

The merit of the total festival wins blessing for the living, *i.e.,* the blessing of new life and renewal for the next generation, and frees the tortured and uncared-for souls in the underworld. Not only the world of the living but also the underworld of the dead are renewed and liberated from the bonds of suffering and calamity.

## A Festival of Renewal

The themes of the *Chiao* are, therefore, many. In its basic sense, the purpose of the festival is to provide community rebirth and renewal. A cycle of sixty years or so has passed. Just as nature is annually reborn at the time of the winter solstice, so the greater cosmos must be renewed for a greater cycle of man's lifetime. Just as the sun, the great *Yang*, is reborn annually, and *Yin*, the "great darkness," after reaching its zenith begins to yield to light and life, so man must restore himself and be assured that babies will be born, crops will flourish, and nature will give blessings for the coming generations. The basic theme of the *Chiao* is to restore *Yang*, that is, life, light, and blessing, to its pristine state of growth, and to expel the forces of *Yin*, darkness, evil, and death.

The word *Chiao* originally meant the offering of wine and incense in respect. It can be found in the forty-third and forty-fourth chapters of the *Book of Rites*, referring to the *Kuan* ritual performed for a boy at puberty; it was also used to describe a part of the wedding ceremony, when the young couple was offered a cup of wine upon entering the ancestral hall. As early as the *Han Shu,* in the twenty-fifth chapter, *P'an Ku* used the word to mean a sacrifice offered to the spirits. *Liu Chih-wan* of the *Academia Sinica* has carefully traced the history of the word from the beginning of religious Taoism until the present in his recently published work *Great Propitiatory Rites of Petition*, the English title for his work on the *Chiao* festival.[6] The word is, therefore, ancient; almost from the beginning of the history of church Taoism, *Chiao* was used to refer to the great ritual of renewal performed by the priests of orthodox Heavenly Master sect Taoism. The various preparations for the *Chiao*, the acts of purification, repentance, abstinence from meat, and so forth, derive from Han dynasty religious practices, in common use among the Chinese farming villages.[7]

## The *Chiao* Demands Purification

In preparing for the festival, the earth spirits are first removed from the temple to make way for the Heavenly Worthies, the spirits who dwell in the Prior Heavens, the realm of pure *Yang*. Their presence is necessary in order to effect the renewal of the cosmos and to bring down the blessings desired from the rituals of the *Chiao*. Since the heavenly spirits are associated with purity, and lack of any taint or hint of the influences of *Yin,* the men of the community must begin to purify themselves and avoid activities or objects which might impede the coming of the spirits. Abstinence from meat, bathing, and almsgiving are considered to be appropriate activities for winning merit and attaining the ends sought in the festival proceedings. The accumulated merits of the *Chiao*, the acts of purification, almsgiving, repair of the temple, the offering of ritual by the Taoists, and finally the *P'u-tu* banquet on the last day, win blessing for the coming life cycle and free the souls of the underworld in a general amnesty. But preliminary to all of the rites and activities of the festival are acts which free men from impurity resulting from *Yin*.

Purification has a social and a personal aspect. The taboo on slaughtering of animals and on articles of clothing deriving from animals is enforced by the temple committee. Woolen or leather clothes are not permitted. The color white, associated with the direction west and death, cannot be worn into the temple. Meat is simply not sold in the village butcher shops for a week before the proceedings begin, nor is the cooking of meat allowed until the final day of the *Chiao* festival, before the *P'u-tu* banquet for freeing the souls.

The *Chiao* begins to set past wrongs in order by decreeing acts of merit and repentance to be performed by the whole community. Just as virtuous acts and pleasant talk were encouraged during the New Year festival, so acts of filial piety, reciprocal obligations, the repayment of debts, and other such social virtues are encouraged before the *Chiao* begins and throughout the days of the festival. One must set right all wrongs, before thinking of rebirth or renewal.

In addition to socially oriented purification, there must be individual cleansing as well. The cessation of marital relations during the festival, the abstention from meat and fine foods, and the taboo on wearing white underwear are strictly enforced for all those who will enter the temple during the ritual performances. Guards at the temple door check to see that the taboos are being observed.

## The *Chiao* Demands Acts of Merit and Repentence

The *Chiao's* purpose of renewal and purification cannot be attained unless numerous acts of merit and repentance are performed by the entire community. The Chinese concept of sin is analogous to guilt and crime, and the Chinese word *Tsui* denotes all three concepts. *Tsui* means sin-guilt-crime, a "chain" definition, as Wolfram Eberhard points out in his work

*Guilt and Sin in Traditional China.*[8] Bad deeds are like debts which must be repaid in the fiery world of the afterlife. In funereal ritual, the Taoist is called upon to lead the soul through the ten stages of punishment that comprise hell.[9] He summons all his magical powers to help the soul pass through the various stages and pays bribes of mock money to the demons and the judges on the way. He also reads endless canons of merit and repentance, called literally *"Tso Kung-te,"* performing works of merit, and *Ch'an,* canonical texts of repentance. So, too, in the *Chiao* ceremony the Taoist must read endless canons of merit and repentance. Thus, guilt of the people of the community is alleviated, preparing them for the blessings of rebirth and renewal to be received from the spirits of the Prior Heavens. Also, the souls suffering in the underworld, especially the orphan souls and the wandering spirits without ancestors to care for them or a tablet to localize their worship, are thus freed by the accumulated wealth of the community's merit.

On the part of the people, deeds which accumulate merit include the giving of money to the temple for repairs and for the expenses of the *Chiao* festival; the giving of alms to the poor and the crippled, who flock into each village throughout Taiwan during the festival in order to receive monetary gifts; the giving of a banquet on the last day of the *Chiao* called the *P'u-tu,* or the general amnesty; and the attendance at the *Chiao* rituals when the canons of merit and repentance are chanted by the priests inside and outside the temple.

Much of the sickness and the natural calamities which befall the village community is thought to be caused by orphan souls, who lead a life of lonely starvation in the afterworld, waiting to prey upon men for neglecting them.[10] A bad crop or a financial loss is often blamed on the fact that an overly frugal village has not offered a *Chiao* for a long time and that the orphan souls have been allowed to accumulate. Heaven's blessing is thus associated with acts of merit and repentance that alleviate the suffering of the untended souls in the netherworld who harm the visible world of man.

The *Chiao,* moreover, includes many themes in ritual acts which precede and are an integral part of the festival. These include rituals of symbolic rebirth, purification, and acts of penitential merit and repentance. The giving of a huge banquet on the last day symbolizes the consummation of the renewal, the awarding of all blessings to the future generations of mortals, and the releasing of all the souls of those who lived in the past from further punishment in the underworld. The focal point is the present, the immediate village community, which for the period of the *Chiao* festival has become the center of the universe. The spirits of the Prior Heavens, bearers of life and blessing, have come into the microcosm of man's life and surroundings to cause blessing and renewal, a blessing which extends to the entire cosmos. The baleful spirits of the underworld have been freed in a general amnesty, and the village is to prosper for another generation.

## The Taoist Entourage

In order to perform a *Chiao* festival, the temple committee must hire a troupe of Taoist priests to perform the intricate rituals of renewal. In Taiwan there are two kinds of Taoists: the *Yü Fu* or Jade Prefecture class, who are known to the people as "Black-head" Taoists, and the *Shen-hsiao* or Spirit-cloud class, who are called "Red-head." Both classes perform the *Chiao* ceremonies, but the differences between the two orders are striking. The Black-head Taoists called themselves "orthodox," and their tradition derives from the mainland headquarters of southern Taoism, Lung-hu Shan in Kiangsi province, on the mainland. The head of the monastic group, who lives in a little village near Lung-hu Shan (Dragon-Tiger Mountain),[11] claims to be the descendant of the founder of Heavenly Master sect church Taoism at the end of the Han dynasty. The 63rd-generation descendant moved to Taiwan in the early nineteen-fifties and, having recently passed away, has been succeeded by a male relative, the 64th-generation Heavenly Master. The Black-heads claim to have been ordained into the orthodox Heavenly Master sect tradition. Their manner of performing the *Chiao* is above reproach, exquisite, and extremely expensive. In north Taiwan, a Taoist costs the equivalent of $500 U.S. for a three-day festival, and as much as $800 for a five-day performance. The *Chiao* festival celebrated in Chung-Kang ward of Chu Nan city, in Miaoli county, north of Taiwan, in December, 1970, lasted for five days. The price paid to the orthodox Heavenly Master sect Taoist high priest for his performance was $30,000 Taiwanese, the equivalent of $750 U.S.

The Red-head Taoists are not as expensive, and their ritual performances are not as expertly done. In general, the Red-heads tend to be more dramatic and popular, the Black-heads more stately and reverent. Some of the differences may be seen in the illustrations, selected from both Red-head and Black-head *Chiao* performances in Taiwan. To the Black-head Taoists, the Red-heads are heterodox, even if their avowed purposes in performing the *Chiao* rituals are the same as those of the Black-heads.

After a Taoist with his entourage has been hired, the high priest, in this case *Chuang-ch'en*, must sublease the various performances to his disciples and friends. Taoists collaborate with each other in a sense of traditional camaraderie. Many of *Chuang's* peers were ordained Taoists and received their training under *Chuang's* father and grandfather, who were famous Taoist masters. *Chuang* ranged from Taipei in the north of the island to as far south as Kaohsiung to find helpers. In all, fourteen Taoists were hired to perform the various ceremonies.

The *Chiao* rituals are divided into three general classifications. The first class, the elite *K'o-i* ritual (that is, alternating ritual),[12] is usually performed behind the locked doors of the temple. Only the village elders, the committee members, and the family sponsoring the lamp to the particular deity being honored are allowed to watch. *Chuang*, assisted by four other Taoists, performed these rituals himself, with one-third of the stipend going to *Chuang*, and the other two-thirds shared equally among the four assistants. Since two of the assistants were his sons, the *Chuang* family stood to profit from the venture. The four musicians who participated in the ritual inside the temple were each paid $160 Taiwanese, that is, about $4 U.S. a day.

The second kind of ritual consists of the canons of merit and repentance. These are read endlessly day and night, inside the temple; the very reading of the texts is thought to win forgiveness for misdemeanors and to accumulate merit for the village community.[13] The canons are chanted by one or another of the disciples and have been allotted to me to perform upon occasion.

The third kind of ritual is performed in public for all to see. Such rites are often highly dramatized, and have catechetical value for the villagers who appreciate and enjoy the performance. In this classification are the minor rites which the Taoists perform in private homes for the sake of the village community. Thus, the nine remaining Taoists hired to help in the *Chiao* ceremonies spent all three days of the festival visiting every family in the village, blessing the homes, and offering food to the gods in the huge *T'an* structures set up around town. For these services, they were remunerated by stipends from individual families and not by the temple committee or the chief Taoist. The Taoists hired to perform the exterior rituals occasionally relieved the Taoists inside the temple, for the pace of the interior rituals was indeed grueling. At such times they were remunerated by the temple committee, according to the wage scale indicated above.

## Preparing the Temple

In order to perform the *Chiao* rituals the Taoist entourage must first reconstitute the temple after the interior of a Taoist monastery, which is itself modeled on the mandala of the Prior Heavens. The gods of the popular religion, having been removed to benches by the entrance of the temple (*i.e.,* the south side, from which place the faithful usually worship), the Taoists fill the interior of the temple with scrolls depicting the gods and Heavenly Worthies of the Prior Heavens. As the gods of the people's religion "belong to the people," so the people enjoy a special prerogative to worship the gods of the Taoists.

The gods whom the common people worship (the patron spirits of Chinese religion) are the gods of the visible world, known in Taoist terminology as the "Posterior Heavens," where change takes place. These gods are divided into three stages, the heavens, the world of nature around man, and the underworld hidden beneath the mountains and the ocean. The three stages of the visible world are governed by the movements of the seasons, and the revolving rule of the two principles of change, *Yin* and *Yang*. The spirits of the three stages are removed from the inner temple during the *Chiao* rituals.

The gods whom the Taoists worship are resident in stellar constellations, known in technical terms as the Prior Heavens, the abode of the eternal, transcendent *Tao*. The Prior Heavens are exempt from the changes of *Yin* and *Yang* and are the sources of life, primordial breath, and blessing in the world of the Posterior Heavens. It is the duty of the Taoist to renew the village and the cosmos by calling these spirits into the village temple and into the microcosm of the body. But the villagers, the devout believers in the folk religion, are unaware of the more subtle and esoteric meanings of the Taoist meditations and are cognizant only of the dramatic rituals going on before their eyes.

The Taoists, therefore, set up the temple after a model of the Prior Heavens. Along the north wall of the temple are hung scrolls to the Three Pure Ones, the highest of the Taoist divinities. These are the Primordial Heavenly Worthy, Lord of Heaven; the *Ling-pao* Heavenly Worthy, Lord of Earth; and the *Tao-te* Heavenly Worthy, also known as Lord *Lao*, the Lord of Man. Their residences are in the three highest of the heavenly realms and in the head of man, which is the part of the microcosm corresponding to the heavens. Their offices or spheres of domination are over the *Ni Huan* or Yellow Court in the head of man, the Red Palace or heart of man, and the Cinnabar Field in the abdomen, respectively. Thus macrocosm and microcosm are seen to correspond to the temple when prepared for Taoist liturgy.

In the center of the temple the Taoist imagines the *Lo Shu,* that is, the eight trigrams of the *Book of Changes*, as conceived by King *Wen*. The five directions, east, south, west, north, and center, are taken to represent symbolically the five sacred peaks of China, T'ai Shan in the east, Heng Shan in the south, Hua Shan in the west, another Heng Shan in the north, and

Sung Shan in the center. The interstices are the gate of heaven in the northwest, the gate of earth in the southwest, the entrance of man in the southeast, and the devil's door in the northeast. The Taoist will seal the devil's door and open heaven's gate, in order to forbid the entrance of the forces of *Yin* and bring down primordial *Yang* from the Prior Heavens. The temple, as the Taoist envisions it, resembles the floor plan in Figure 1.

# NORTH

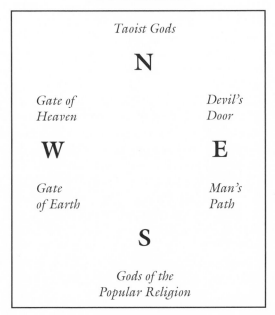

# SOUTH

Figure 1. The floor plan of the temple as the Taoist prepares for the ritual performance.

The east wall of the temple is then hung with three scrolls, representing the bureau of heavenly spirits, the bureau of earthly spirits, and the Dragon General *K'ang Yüan-shuai*, representing the forces of *Yang*. The west wall of the temple is also hung with three scrolls, representing the bureau of fire spirits, the bureau of water spirits, and the Tiger General *Chao Yüan-shuai*, representing the forces of *Yin*.

In the middle of the temple area, directly in front of the main temple altar, the Taoists place a table. On the table is a special incense bowl, which will be carried in processions and in which will be burned the various memorials which the Taoists send up to heaven. On the east side of the table is a large brass bowl representing *Yang*. When struck, its mellow tones reverberate through the temple, filling the area with the rich sounds of *Yang* and life. On the west side of the table is placed a large, hollow, wooden sphere, called the "wooden fish" *(Mu Yü)*. This instrument is also sounded during the ritual performances, and its hollow, muted tone fulfills the role of *Yin*.

The Taoist high priest, called *Kao-kung Fa-Shih*, "Master of Exalted Merit," stands in the very center of the area, directly in front of the table, with the ritual manual open in front of him, from which he sings the particular rite. To his right, playing the role of *Yang* and sounding the brass bowl or bell, is the *Tu Chiang*, the chief cantor. To the left of the high priest, playing the role of *Yin* and sounding the wooden fish, is the *Fu Chiang*, or assistant cantor. The chief cantor and assistant cantor alternate in singing the words of the text, thus giving the name *K'o-i* or "alternating" rites to the liturgy. The name, of course, symbolizes the alternating roles of *Yin* and *Yang* in the universe, which are dramatized by the singing of the priests.

The vestments which the Taoist priests wear are filled with embroidered symbolism. The high priest in the center wears a huge, red vestment called *Chiang-i* or "vestment of descent." Since the word *Chiang* is also a homonym for the color red, a secondary meaning is the "red vestment," for it must traditionally be made of red silk, lined with blue or blue-green. On the back of the vestment in gold thread is embroidered the universe, with Mount K'un-lun in the center, over which stands a three-storied pavilion. The highest three heavens, abode of the Three Pure Ones, are thus symbolically represented by the great robe.

The chief cantor and the assistant cantor wear a knee-length tunic called *Tao P'ao* or Taoist robe, which has in the very center of the back an embroidered representation of the eight trigrams of *Fu Hsi*, the *Pa Kua* of the Prior Heavens. Other themes such as herons, butterflies (after the dream of *Chuang-tzu*), and *Ch'i-lin* (a mythical beast like a unicorn) adorn the red silk garment in fancy proliferation. The sleeves and lower part of the tunic are of green silk, and the eight trigrams are embroidered as a stole in front. The official belt of a mandarin, called *Chiao Tai* or "horned belt," is embroidered around the center, showing that the Taoist is a heavenly official, mediator between the rule of the gods and man.

On their heads the Taoists wear a black skullcap, woven either of human or horse hair. The cap is symbolic of the topknot which was the trade mark of Taoists in the past, who traditionally wore their hair tied in a knot atop the head. A small, gold crown, which is made of carved wood and is studded with cut-glass jewels, graces the very top of the cap. The cap and gold crown represent the heavens and the stars, for the Taoist, when wearing it, stands in the highest heavens before the Heavenly Worthies. The top of the crown is also painted with the eight trigrams, and the name of the whole ensemble is *Chin K'uan*, the gold crown. The word *K'uan* or crown is used to describe the headpiece of an official, demonstrating that the Taoist is a mandarin in the offices of the heavenly rulers. To the common folk, therefore, a Taoist is by definition a mandarin official of the spirits.

Finally, from the top of the chief Taoist's crown there emanates a flame-shaped, metal pin painted gold, with a small, round mirror in the center. The flame-pin is called *Yang*, or "apex," and is symbolic of the fact that the Taoist high priest, the *Kao-kung Fa-shih*, is lighted from within by the fire of the eternal *Tao*. The flame-pin is inserted into the crown of the headpiece during the first part of each orthodox ritual precisely when the incense is lit, at the point when the Taoist begins to construct in his imagination the mandala of the Prior Heavens. The Taoist is seen as the mediator of life-renewing forces. Standing in the center of the cosmos, he is alive and burning with the transcendent *Tao* of the *Wu Wei* (as opposed to the immanent *Tao* of the *Yu Wei*, the *Tao* of change in the Posterior Heavens). The fire of new life springing from the crown on top of his head will relight the universe with the powers of *Yang*, and all blessing.

## The Rituals of the *Chiao*

The rituals are now ready to begin. The overall plan of the *Chiao* can be seen from the following list of the rituals, posted on a wall of the temple for the public to examine.

### *The First Day*

1. The *Fa Piao* (midnight). The Taoists send off a huge memorial written on red paper, announcing to all the spirits of the three stages of the world that the *Chiao* is to be held.

2. *Ch'ing Shen*, inviting the heavenly spirits. The Taoists invite the Heavenly Worthies into the sacred area to attend the *Chiao* ritual and grant rebirth and blessing.

3. *Kua Pang*, "Raising the Standards." In front of the temple three bamboo poles are erected. In the presence of the public the Taoists raise three standards and three lanterns. The center pole bears the standard of the Jade Emperor; the left pole *(Yang)* bears the standard and lantern of the

seven Pole Stars; the right pole *(Yin)* bears the standard and lantern of the souls in the underworld.

4.    *Chin T'an,* "Purifying the *T'an.*" The Taoists perform an exorcistic rite, which seals the "devil's door" or the northeast position inside the temple. The rite symbolizes that the forces of *Yin* are forbidden entrance.

5.    Reading the canons of merit and repentance. The disciples of the Taoist high priest read the lengthy canons of merit and repentance. For the first morning, these include the following:

    i. North Pole canon *(Pei Tou Ching)*
    ii. South Pole canon *(Nan Ch'en Ching)*
    iii. Jade Pivot canon *(Yü Shu Ching)*
    iv. Three Officials canon *(San Kuan Ching)*

6.    Noon Offering, *Wu Hsien.* The Taoists offer nine objects to the Heavenly Worthies inside the temple: incense, wine, rice, fire, tea, fruit, *man-t'ou* (steamed bread), flowers, and precious things such as jewelry and coins. The rite is repeated in public, in front of the temple and at the various *T'an* around the community, in honor of the visiting spirits.

7.    Canons of merit and repentance. The afternoon is filled with the reading of more canonical texts, including the Canon of the Three Origins, *San Yüan Ching.*

8.    In the evening the *Fen Teng* ceremony, "lighting the new fire" or "lighting the lamps," is performed. During the rite, a new fire is struck, and votive lamps are lit in front of the Three Pure Ones, the highest trinity of spirits in the Taoist hierarchy of the Prior Heavens. The forty-second chapter of the *Lao-tzu* is read during the ceremony: "The Tao gave birth to the One; the One gave birth to the Two; the Two gave birth to the Three."

9.    The *Su Ch'i* ritual, or implanting the five *Ling Pao* "True Writs," is performed near midnight of the first full day of ritual. This is considered to be by far the most important of the rituals of the *Chiao* and the most sacred of the secret ceremonies. In this ritual, the renewal of the community is begun, and the ritual should be seen to be a planting of the five primordial life-giving elements of the Prior Heavens, symbolically represented by the five sacred emperors, into the five directions of the sacred temple area.

### The Second Day

Like the first day, the second and, in fact all of the days of the *Chiao* festival are filled with the readings of canons for merit and repentance. The day begins with a reinviting of the spirits, and then early in the morning, the theme of the second day is introduced in the rite called Morning Audience.

1.    Morning Audience, *Tsao Ch'ao*. The Morning Audience begins between 3:00 and 5:00 in the morning, and is basically an audience with the first of the Three Pure Ones, the Primordial Heavenly Worthy. Its esoteric meaning is not understood by the devout laymen, and very few witness its beauty, due to the early hour and the state of exhaustion of the participants after the rites of the first day. A green document with the petitions of the community is sent off to the heavens.

The first day's program of canonical readings, the noon offering, and so forth are continued on the second day.

The next important rite of the day is the second of the audiences, called the Noon Audience. A red document (noon) is sent off to the heavens, bearing the names and petitions of the community members.

2.    The Noon Audience, *Wu Ch'ao*, begins somewhere between the hours of 9:00 and 11:00 in the morning, and ends at high noon, the center of the day. It celebrates an audience with the second of the Three Heavenly Worthies, the *Ling-pao T'ien Tsun*, Lord of Earth. The Red-head Taoists add to the Noon Audience a series of ritual dances, tracing the stars of the twenty-eight heavenly constellations in the center of the sacred temple area. The rite is well attended by the devout laymen of the community, who are admitted into the purified temple to witness it.

The afternoon of the second day begins to stress the role of the laymen in the *Chiao* festival. After the canonical readings and the noon offering, the Taoists hold the last of the three audiences, the Night Audience. The laymen undertake a grand procession to the sea to "float the lanterns," summoning the souls of the departed for the banquet on the last day.

3.    The Night Audience, *Wan Ch'ao*, is usually scheduled to begin in the late afternoon and to be finished by sunset. It is an audience with the third of the Three Pure Ones, the *Tao-te* Heavenly Worthy, Lord *Lao*, Lord of Men. A yellow document is sent off, by burning, to memorialize the heavens.

4.    Floating the lanterns, *Fang shui teng*. The lengthy afternoon procession to float the lanterns in a nearby stream, or in the ocean, begins to form at about 3:00 p.m. in front of the temple. The families and greater clans, who have sponsored lamps in the temple, now assemble in the plaza, in the same order in which their lamps have been placed inside the temple. Each family is represented by its male members, one of whom (usually the eldest son) carries a paper lantern affixed to a small bamboo raft. The greater clans and the various guilds and factories of the village or city sponsor huge floats covered with lanterns and carrying a band of musicians. A hired truck transports the ensemble. The parade is a mile or so long, and winds in and

out of the village streets, growing as it goes along. As dusk approaches, the participants light kerosene torches, made of bamboo with cotton cloth tied to the end. The procession of torches winds its way to the sea, where the lanterns are released, to float away on the tide, or be carried out to sea on the swiftly flowing waters of a river. The souls from the netherworld are thus summoned for the banquet on the last day.

### The Third Day

The third day begins, as did the preceding days, with the reinviting of the spirits and an early-morning popular rite summoning the Jade Emperor, the head of the spirits of the Posterior Heavens, to the last day's proceedings.

1.  Inviting the Jade Emperor. In a popular ritual the Taoists first pay homage to the Jade Emperor before performing the orthodox rituals of the last day.

2.  *Tao Ch'ang,* mandala of the Prior Heavens, in which a banquet is offered to the Three Pure Ones.[14] The *Tao Ch'ang* completes the rituals of renewal of the *Chiao* festival by bringing together the Three Pure Ones in the center of the village temple and establishing a feudal treaty with the gods of the Prior Heavens.

3.  *Chin Piao.* Presentation of the memorial. With the Three Pure Ones now in the center of the cosmos, the village temple, and the microcosm, the Taoists present the memorial of the community, the *Shu Wen,* to the Heavenly Worthies; the document contains the names of all the villagers, their petitions, and a summation of the rites of the *Chiao* festival.

4.  *Shou Chen-wen.* Continuing the rites of conclusion, the Taoist performs the ritual called "harvesting" or taking back the Five Talismans, the reverse of the *Su Ch'i* ritual on the first day. He recalls the primordial breaths and primordial spirits back into the microcosm of his body.

5.  Public presentation of the memorial. Having finished the orthodox rituals, the Taoists come out to the plaza in front of the temple and perform the "presentation of the memorial" again for all to see. Whereas the memorial was presented to the Three Heavenly Worthies inside the temple, in the exterior ceremony it is presented to the Jade Emperor, with the Taoists, their rituals, and their heavenly spirits as mediators. The rite is also called "Climbing up Mount T'ai [China's most famous religious mountain where the emperors performed the *Feng* and *Shan* sacrifices to heaven and earth] and Preaching the *Tao.*" At the conclusion a great placard called *Pang* is posted on the temple walls, naming all the people of the community who have taken part in the renewal.

6.  The *P'u-tu*, or banquet for the souls in the underworld. On tables set up in front of the temple, the people lay out several acres of food. Each family provides a twenty-four-course banquet for the souls, including ancestors, orphan souls, and wandering demons. The whole village becomes a part of the rite, with a table laden with food placed in front of every residence. Meanwhile, the village has become a carnival, with side shows, local opera, and puppet shows on every street. The Taoists come out in public to perform the *P'u-tu* rite which releases all the souls from hell. The banquet for the human visitors takes place shortly after the *P'u-tu* has ended.

7.  Thanking and seeing off the gods. The last act of the *Chiao* ritual belongs to the Taoists, who are almost alone in the temple to thank the gods who have attended the festival and to send them back to their respective realms. The *Chiao* has now come to an end. The Taoists dismantle the sacred area and pack to return home.

Such, in brief detail, is a description of the *Chiao* festival as the people see it. In their minds renewal of the temple and the rebirth of the village are completed. The souls in the underworld have been released. The community has been drawn together in an immense banquet. The heavens have been engaged in a feudal contract to bless the village for another lifetime. The terrible expense of the festival can truly be borne only once a lifetime, but the extravagances were indeed worth the rewards. Man, like the annual cycle of nature, has spiritually renewed himself for another cycle. Each family takes home a yellow document, bearing the seal of the Taoist, which describes the contract with the heavens; it is hung over the family altar until the next *Chiao* festival of renewal, bearing witness to the gods that the ritual was indeed accomplished.

# III

# The Philosophical Basis of the Ritual of Renewal

The purpose of the *Chiao* festival is village renewal. By what means the Taoists accomplish the renewal, other than by the elaborate rituals going on inside the closed doors of the temple, very few if any of the villagers are cognizant. Just as the common man traditionally leaves the government of the visible world to the mandarins and keeps a respectful distance from bureaucracy and its manipulations, so too the ordinary folk leave the government and manipulation of the gods of the Prior Heavens to their mandarins, the Taoists.

Any inquiry into the sources of Taoist liturgy is difficult. The Taoist preserves his professional knowledge for one son a generation, a legal prescription confirmed by the laws of Imperial China as well as by Taoist tradition. Each Taoist has in his possession a secret manual called *Tao-chiao Yüan-liu,* the "Origins of Religious Taoism." In the book, in cryptic and shortened form, can be found a resumé of religious Taoism. But the original texts can only be guessed at, for the *Tao-chiao Yüan-liu* is but a reminder of lengthier and more systematic passages which the Taoist knows orally. One of the basic texts from which the book is derived is the *Huai-nan-tzu* (ca. 122 B.C.), from which the following three quotations are taken.[1]

*On the Origin of Tao (from the Huai-nan-tzu)*
*Chapter One*

*Tao* fills the heavens and supports the earth.
It extends to the four quarters, and touches the extremes of the eight directions
Its height has no limit and its depth cannot be plumbed.
It contains within itself heaven and earth, and endows that which has no form.
It is an origin from which a spring wells up, bubbles, and begins to overflow.
The turbid chaos seethes and begins to clear.
Therefore it established and filled heaven and earth.

Penetrating, it was given to the four seas; used, it never could be exhausted.
No sunrise and sunset to *Tao*.
Scattered far and wide, it filled heaven, earth, everywhere.
Rolled up and grasped in the hand, there was not enough for a squeeze.

(2a-1)

*Tao* can be concise, but stretched quite long; dark, but shine brightly; weak, but become strong.
Nothing that does not respond to the *Tao*.
It is the axle of the four seasons.
It contains *Yin* and *Yang*,
Binding together the universe.
Making bright the three sources of light.
It is very thick and congealed, very delicate and refined.
Because of it, mountains are tall, and the sea is deep; animals walk, and birds fly;
The sun and moon are bright, and the heavens move; the unicorn comes forth, and phoenix soars.
Long ago, in the very beginning, the two emperors [ *Yin* and *Yang*], having attained the *Tao's* authority, were established in the center. Their spirits then spread far and wide, ruling the four directions.
This is why the heavens move and the earth is stable.
Turning and revolving without exhaustion.

(2b-1)

Water flows, never stopping, coterminus with the myriad creatures,
Winds blow, clouds rise, all is as it should be.
Thunder sounds and rain falls, always responding, never tiring.
Like the traces which a demon leaves or lightning's entrance,
Dragon's rising, phoenix's landing;
Like a potter's wheel, revolving round, returning to the starting point;
Now carving, now polishing, it returns to the origin, it is like the uncarved block of wood.
Doing the *"Wu Wei"* [*i.e.,* moving like heaven without using up primordial *"Yang"* breath] attains to unity with *Tao*.
Speaking the *"Wu Wei"* attains to the *"Te."*
No desires, no pride, attain to harmony [with the *Tao*].
No concern over the myriad creatures, and one's nature will change [to be like the *Tao*].
One's *shen* spirit will touch even the smallest things, and be big enough to penetrate and unite the cosmos.
One's virtue [ *Te*] will support heaven and earth, and harmonize with *Yin* and *Yang*;
Divide the four seasons, and order the five elements,
Warm and nourish the myriad creatures and all living things.
Like the *Tao* moisten grass and trees, immerse metal and stone, fatten birds and animals, polish pelt and quill, strengthen feathered wings and horned creatures.

(3a-1)

[Due to the *Tao*] animals do not miscarry, and eggs are not sterile,
Fathers do not with grief bury their child,
Brothers do not weep for brother's death [ *i.e.,* because brothers do not die an untimely death],
Children are not orphaned, nor wives widowed,
The evil rainbow does not appear and unlucky stars do not harm; it is possessing the power of the *Tao* which stops them [and wins blessing].

## On the Heavens

*Chapter Three*

The name of heaven and earth, before it was formed,
When it was still an empty void, and murky darkness, was the Great Origin.
The *Tao* gave birth to this Great Void.
The Great Void gave birth to the *"Yü-chou"* cosmos [*Yü* is heaven, earth, and the four
    directions; *Chou* is the perspective of time, from origin to present].
From the cosmos was born primordial breath,
Which has its upper reaches and its lower roots.
The pure and bright [*Yang*] part of it wafted upwards and formed the heavens;
The heavy and turbid part of it congealed downwards and made the earth.
The pure and bright's joining and revolving was easy; but the heavy and turbid's congealing
    was hard;
Therefore the heavens were formed first,
And afterwards earth was established.
Heaven and earth united their breath and made *Yin* and *Yang*.
*Yin* and *Yang* revolved their breath and caused the four seasons;
The four seasons scattered the purified breath and produced the myriad creatures.
The warm primordial-breath of *Yang* when amassed
Gives birth to fire; fire's breath purified into seminal breath gives birth to the sun.
The cold breath of *Yin* when amassed produces water;
Water's breath when purified into seminal breath produces the moon.
The stars and planets were products of the unpurified seminal breath of sun and moon.
Heaven received sun, moon, stars, and planets;
Earth received gushing water and dusty soil.
Long long ago *Kung Kung* and *Chuan Hsü* fought over who was to be king.
In their rage they dashed against Pu Shou Mountain.

(2b-1)

So that the heavenly pillar broke, and the earthly cord was cut. The heavens listed to the
    northwest, and so the sun, moon, and stars move in that direction.
The earth was torn up to the southeast, and thus water and soil return to that direction.
The *Tao* of heaven is round.
The *Tao* of earth is square.
The square is ruler of the "dark,"
The round is master of the "bright."
The bright breathes forth [exhales] primordial breath;
Thus fire gives forth brightness.
The dark breathes in primordial breath, and thus it "takes brightness inside" to itself.
That which breathes forth the primordial life breath causes that which consumes life breath to
    change.
Thus *Yang* causes *Yin* to transform.

(4b-2)

Man's control over his breath is connected to the heavens above.
Cruel punishment means violent winds;
Useless vain laws bring blight and pestilence;
Gross slaughter causes the earth of the country to be scorched.
Timely orders not obeyed mean terrible floods.
The four seasons are heaven's chronicler;
The sun and moon are heaven's messengers;

Stars and planets are heaven's assent;
Rainbow and comets are heaven's "no."
The heavens are nine in number. 9,999 Li high, mutually extended over all the earth's nooks
    and crannies, its width 50,000 billion Li.
There are five stars, eight winds, and twenty-eight stellar  constellations.

## On Seminal Breath and Spirit

*Chapter Seven*

Of old, before heaven and earth,
There was neither shape nor form.
Over all was darkness and obscurity, *"Yao-yao Ming-ming,"*
Formless, shapeless, *"Hsiang-meng Hung-tung,"*
No way of knowing what was its portal.
Then two spirits joined and gave birth, tiered the heavens and formed the earth,
So deep that one could not fathom its depths,
So vast that one could not know its limits.
Thereupon the two spirits separated and became *Yin* and *Yang.*
Scattered they caused the eight directions;
The hard and the soft [*Yang* and *Yin*] mutually united,
Formed and gave shape to the myriad things.
Sullied life breath became crawling creatures;
Purified life-breath became man.

(2a-1)

This is why purified [seminal] breath and spirit are heaven's;
Bones and limbs belong to earth.
Seminal breath and spirit enter their proper gate [heaven];
Bones and limbs return to their roots [earth].
How is it, then, that I exist?
It is due to the fact that the holy man's rule is to follow heaven,
His passions are not ensnared in the vulgar, nor is he tempted by the [wiles of] man.
Heaven is his father, and earth his mother;
*Yin* and *Yang* are his bonds,
The four seasons are his rule.
Heaven in its being quiet is pure;
Earth in its being stable is at peace.
The myriad creatures in losing [this principle] die,
In taking it as their rule, are born.
Bright spirit dwells in the still and the deep;
The *Tao's* abode is the transcendent void.
Thus those who seek it outside lose it within,
And those who keep it within lose it outside.
It is like the roots and branches of a tree;
From the roots come the many branches and myriad leaves;
There is nothing which does not follow this rule.
Purified [seminal] breath and spirit are the gift of heaven;
Bodily shape is the endowment of earth.
Thus is it said that the "One gives birth to the Two; the Two gives birth to the Three; the Three
    gave birth to the myriad creatures," [The "one" is heaven; the "Two" is earth; the "Three"
    is the union with primordial breath, seminal essence, and spirit, *i.e.,* man. Or, the "One"
    is the primordial breath; the "Two" seminal essence; heaven and earth produce *Yin* and
    *Yang*, which united with the Primordial Spirit produce the "Three," man.]

The myriad creatures bear *Yin* on their backs and *Yang* in their stomachs.
The blending [of the two] with Primordial [Spirit] breath causes their harmonious union.
Thus, in the first month, embryo;
In the second month, swelling;
In the third month, the womb shows;

(2b-1)

In the fourth month, limbs;
In the fifth month, sinews;
In the sixth month, bones;
In the seventh month, completed!
In the eighth month, it moves!
In the ninth month, it stretches;
In the tenth month, born!
The body's shape is thus formed, and the five viscera molded.
This is why the lungs [outgoing fire, red, south] regulate the eyes;
The kidneys [turtle, water, north, breath-circulating] govern the nose;
The gall [courage] governs the mouth;
The liver [gold, fire inside] governs the ears. [The text is corrupt here. "The spleen governs the tongue" is omitted; in 3a-11 it is included.]
The exterior organs are but an expression of that which is within.
  Opening and closing, stretching and gathering itself together, each has its coming and going [*i.e.,* its going forth and its arriving].
Thus the head is round, the shape of heaven, and the feet are square, shaped to the earth.

(3a-1)

The heavens have four seasons, five elements, and nine divisions, with 366 days. Man also has four limbs, five viscera, nine orifices, and 366 sections.
Heaven has wind, rain, cold, and heat;
Man too has a "taking in" and a "giving out"; joy and anger.
Thus the gall corresponds to clouds; the lungs are vapor breath; the liver is wind; the kidneys are rain; and the spleen is thunder.

(3b-1)

Thereby man, heaven, and earth, all three, are mutually related, with the heart as master.
Thus ears and eyes are sun and moon,
Blood and breath are wind and rain.
In the sun there is a three-legged crow, and in the moon a [three legged] toad.
If the sun and moon lose their way, there will be an eclipse and no light.
When wind and rain come out of season, then life is destroyed by calamity and misfortune.
When the five stars lose their proper course, then continent and city-state would bear great disaster.
The *Tao* of heaven and earth expands and is great; nevertheless, it is frugal with its regulated light, and cherishes its bright spirit life.
How can ear and eye work long and hard, and never rest?
How can seminal breath and spirit gallop on without being exhausted?
Thus blood and life breath are [cause of] man's flourishing, while the five organs contain man's purified [seminal] breath.
If the blood and the breath are able to pass into the

(4a-1)

Five organs, and not be dissipated without, then breast and belly are full, and desires are quelled;
Eyes and ears are clear, seeing and hearing acute;

Clear eyes and ears, acute seeing and hearing, is called *"ming"* [bright, intelligence].

When the five organs are ruled by the heart [mind] and are not perverse, then a regulated will overcomes, and does that which is not evil.

When a regulated will overcomes and does not do evil,

Then seminal breath and spirit flourish, and life breath is not dissipated. When seminal breath and spirit flourish and life breath is not dissipated, then there is order.

Order brings regularity like the potter's wheel, regularity brings *"t'ung"* [*Tao* penetrates]; from *"t'ung,"* spirit is influenced, from spirit comes a vision in which nothing is not seen, a hearing in which nothing is not heard, a doing and nothing which is not accomplished. Thus sorrow and grief find no entrance, and evil breath cannot invade. Therefore he who seeks the *Tao* beyond the four seas does not find it, and he who looks for it in the bodily form will not see it.

It is thus that those who seek many things receive few, and those who look for big things know only the small!

Fu! The pores of the body are the doors and windows of seminal breath and spirit; life breath and blood are servants and messengers of the five organs.

(4b-1)

When ear and eye are seduced by sensual pleasure of sound and color, then the five organs are shaken and unstable. When the five organs are shaken and unstable, then breath and blood [will] overflow and are wasted, never resting; when breath and blood overflow and are wasted, never resting, then seminal breath and spirit gallop forth unbridled and are not kept within.

When seminal breath and spirit gallop forth unbridled and are not kept within, then concerning the arrival of calamity and blessing, though big as a mountain, there is no way of knowing whence either one comes, or what caused them.

Thus let the earth and eyes be pure and clear; the dark void is penetrated, and there are no enticing desires. When breath and desires are quelled, then the five organs, also peaceful and at rest, are full and yet not overflowing. The seminal breath and spirit keep to the bodily form and do not wander about outside. When such is the case, then the past can be looked forward to, and the future looked back on, and even then there is far more that could be accomplished! Can one not steer a straight course between calamity and blessing!

Thus it is said that he who wanders far abroad knows but little, thereby explaining why seminal breath and spirit must not be slave to external debauchery.

(5a-5)

Therefore the five colors confuse the eyes, causing the eyes not to see clearly; the five sounds reverberate, causing the ears to be deafened; the five flavors upset the mouth, causing the taste buds to be injured. Inclination and disaffection upset the heart, causing it to walk a harmful path.

Nevertheless these four things [eyes, ears, mouth, heart] are the means by which all under heaven is nourished and thus involve all men. Thus is it said, lusty desires cause man to lose his life breath, love and hate cause man's heart to be sick.

If they are not quickly dispelled then "will" and "life breath" will be daily dissipated.

What is the reason why men are not able to run the full course of their lives? Why does fate cause an early death by criminal punishment or by war? He uses up his life who lives too fully;

If only he could not use his life up in acting; then he would gain long-lasting birth [*Ch'ang sheng*].

(6b-8)

Grief and joy are virtue's ruin; happiness and rage make the *Tao* pass one by.

Love and hate make the heart tired.

Thus is it said, one's birth is heaven moving; one's death is creature's transforming.

(7a-1)

Quiet, at one with *Yin's* virtue [*Tao* possessing].
Acting, moving, at one with *Yang's* moving [*Tao* giving].
When seminal breath and spirit are placid and not exhausted, not dissipated by giving
themselves up to creatures, then all under heaven is of itself submissive [to the *Tao*]. Thus
heart is ruler of the body, and spirit is the precious possession of heart.
When the body is overworked and doesn't revitalize itself, then there is a tumbling and a fall.
When seminal breath is used and not restored, then there is *"ch'ieh,"* exhaustion.
Thus the sagely man prizes it and respects it [seminal breath] and does not let it flow away.

(7b-1)

The realized man is the person whose nature is one with the *Tao!*

The above quotations, which possess an almost mystical quality, express
the fundamental ideals of religious Taoism. Similar ideas are contained in
the Taoist training manual (the *Tao-chiao Yüan-liu*), which every Taoist
possesses. But the text of the *Huai-nan-tzu,* compiled in the court of *Liu
An,* the Prince of Huai-nan, some time before his death in 122 B.C., was
written before the development of the doctrine of the Three Pure Ones, one
of the basic tenets of religious Taoism. In the next the words seminal breath
occur again and again, whereas in later Taoist texts the two become separate.
Thus primordial breath and seminal essence, with spirit, become the three
basic principles of life within man (the microcosm), as well as within the total
cosmos. The text of the *Huai-nan-tzu* only hints at this later development
when it quotes the forty-second chapter of the *Lao-tzu,* "The *Tao* gives birth
to the One; the One gives birth to the Two; the Two gives birth to the
Three."

## The Doctrine of the Three Pure Ones

It is with the founding of the religious Taoist movements, shortly after
100 A.D., that the doctrine of the Three Pure Ones, lords of heaven, earth,
and man, is accepted as a basic doctrine of what will become the Heavenly
Master Taoist movement. In an early Taoist text, called "The Rules and
Regulations of the Orthodox One Heavenly Master Sect," *Chang Tao-ling*
is said to have received the doctrine of the three primordial spirits, *Hsüan,
Yüan,* and *Shih,* and to have spread the new doctrine far and wide.[2]

The *Tao* gives forth a subtle breath
The colors of which are three:
*Hsüan* [dark], *Yüan* [primordial], *Shih* [origin].
The *Hsüan* is blue-green, and formed the heavens.
The *Yüan* is yellow and made the earth.

The *Shih* is white, and is the *Tao* [of man].
From the center, the three breaths rule heaven and earth.
They are the father and the mother of the myriad creatures.
Therefore they are preeminently worthy, preeminently spirits.
Throughout the heavens and the earth, there is nothing
Which does not receive these breaths,
And thereby not be reborn.

All things that are long-lived,
Are able to preserve [within] the *Tao*,
Bear within themselves primordial breath,
Possess seminal essence and spirit,
Exhale and inhale *Yin* and *Yang*.
The *Tao* gives birth to heaven;
Heaven gives birth to earth;
Earth gives birth to man.
All things because of these three primordial breaths,
Are born.

The text goes on to say that by receiving these three spirits into the microcosm one becomes a child of the *Tao*. The *Tao* as eternal principle, then, produces three spirits, principles of heaven, earth, and man. As principles of life within man they are made into persons symbolizing primordial breath, spirit, and seminal essence. As rules of the macrocosm, they are lord of heaven, lord of earth, and lord of man, respectively. The text adds that the Yellow Turban rebellion (suppressed in 185 A.D.) failed because it was a political movement. Its leaders assumed the titles of the Three Pure Ones and attempted to found an earthly regime. The heavenly Master sect on the other hand set up a spiritual rule, based on the doctrine of the Three Pure Ones.

It should be pointed out that the main rituals of the *Chiao* festival described so briefly above were precisely concerned with the Three Pure Ones. The Lighting of the New Fire on the first evening, the Three Audiences during the second day, and, finally, the *Tao Ch'ang* on the last day were rituals whose purpose was to summon the Three Pure Ones into the microcosm, and into the village community, in order to effect renewal.

## The Doctrine of the Five Primordial Spirits

The second set of spirits typifying the rites of religious Taoism is of even greater antiquity than the doctrine of the Three Pure Ones. The title of *Chuang* and his colleagues (orthodox Black-head "Jade Pavilion" Taoists) is *San-wu Tu-kung*, "Three-Five Surveyors of Merit." This title refers to the list of spirits over which they have control, a list which is called the "Orthodox One Auspicious Alliance Three-Five Register." It is, of course, a list of the spirits who dwell in the Prior Heavens, and who are summoned during every orthodox ritual. At the beginning of each rite, the Taoist lights the incense and, while the great ritual drum is sounded twenty-four times (3 x 8 beats of the drum), begins to summon from the microcosm of his own body (as well as from the macrocosm) the gods of the Prior Heavens. The most important of these gods are the Three Pure Ones, lords of heaven, earth, and man. They are also lords of the head, the chest, and the belly in man, corresponding to primordial breath, spirit, and seminal essence. Thus the term "three" in the title of the Taoist is clear.

After the Three Pure Ones, the most important of the spirits are the "five," the second part of the "Three-Five Surveyors of Merit" title. The spirits referred to in the Taoist's title correspond to the five primordials, wood in the east, fire in the south, metal in the west, water in the north, and earth (soil) in the center. Once again the *Huai-nan-tzu* explains who these gods are:

The east is wood; its spirit-emperor is *Fu Hsi*.
Its instrument is the compass [round, like heaven],
Its minister-spirit is *Chü Mang*.
The spring is its domain.
Its spirit is the *Sui* star [Jupiter].
Its animal the blue dragon.
The musical note is *Chiao*.
The cyclical day is *Chia*.

The south is fire; its spirit-emperor is *Shen Nung*,
Whose minister-spirit is *Chu Jung*.
The instrument is the scales,
The summer is its domain.
The star-spirit is *Ying-huo* [Mars].
The animal is the red bird.
The musical note is *Chih*.
And the cyclical day is *Ping-ting*.

The center is earth [soil]; its spirit-emperor is *Huang-ti*.
The minister-spirit is *Hou-t'u* [god of the soil].
The instrument is the cord.
Its domain is the four *"fang"* [the four in-between months].
The star-spirit is *Chen-hsing* [Saturn].
The animal is the yellow dragon,
The musical note is *Kung*.
And the cyclical day is *Wu-chi*.

The west is metal; the spirit-emperor is *Shao-hao*,
Whose minister-spirit is *Ju-shou*.
The instrument is the square,
The domain is autumn.
The star-spirit is *T'ai-po* [Venus].

The animal is the white-tiger.
The music note is *Shang*.
And the cyclical day is *Keng-hsin*.

The north is water; the spirit-emperor is *Chuan-hsü*,
Whose minister is *Hsüan-ming*.
The instrument is the weight.
The domain is winter.
The star-spirit is *Ch'en* [Mercury].
The animal is the *Hsüan-wu* [tortoise].
The musical note is *Yü*.
And the cyclical day is *Jen-Kuei*.

The five directions, the five spirits, and the five elements thus are seen to systemize the cosmos. The *Huai-nan-tzu* states that the five elements correspond to the five central organs within man: the liver to wood in the east, the heart to fire in the south, the spleen to earth in the center, the lungs to metal in the west, and the kidneys to water in the north.

The systemization of the five primordials extends to the visible external world as well as to the internal microcosm. The five great peaks of China are considered to be the special receptacles of the spirits of the five directions, sources of the five primordial elements. Thus T'ai Shan is the dwelling place of the spirits in the east. Heng Shan is the mountain of the south. Sung Shan is the central peak. Hua Shan reigns over the west. Finally, another Heng Shan is the mountain of the north. All of the above relationships can be demonstrated in the following table.

| Elements: | Wood | Fire | Earth | Metal | Water |
|---|---|---|---|---|---|
| Direction: | East | South | Center | West | North |
| Emperor: | *Fsu Hsi* | *Shen Nung* | *Huang-ti* | *Shao-hao* | *Chüan-hsü* |
| Assistant: | *Chü Mang* | *Chu Jung* | *Hou-t'u* | *Ju-shou* | *Hsüan-ming* |
| Season: | Spring | Summer | "Fang" | Autumn | Winter |
| Star: | Jupiter | Mars | Saturn | Venus | Mercury |
| Organ: | Liver | Heart | Spleen | Lungs | Kidneys |
| Mountain: | T'ai Shan | Heng Shan | Sung Shan | Hua Shan | Heng Shan |
| Color: | Blue | Red | Yellow | White | Black |

The spirit emperors and their assistants listed in the above table are personifications of the five elements in as much as they give life and blessing.

The five elements, as all of the cosmos, have a *Yin* and *Yang* aspect. During the first part of the year, when nature is growing, the *Yang* aspect is in ascendancy. During the latter part of the year, when crops ripen and nature begins to progress toward winter and death, the *Yin* aspect is in ascendancy. In the passage from the *Huai-nan-tzu* which describes the five elements, the last line of each stanza speaks of the elements as having a cyclical day. Thus, wood belongs to the cyclical day *Chia-i*, fire to *Ping-ting*, and so forth. To the person familiar with Chinese literature, especially the *Hsi-tz'u* commentary on the *I-ching*, the terms are meaningful. One of the ancient ways of counting from one to ten is by means of the ten heavenly stems, as follows:[3]

| | | | | | |
|---|---|---|---|---|---|
| *Chia* | (3) | *I* | (8) | Wood | |
| *Ping* | (7) | *Ting* | (2) | Fire | |
| *Wu* | (5) | *Chi* | (10) | Earth | |
| *Keng* | (9) | *Hsin* | (4) | Metal | |
| *Jen* | (1) | *Kuei* | (6) | Water | |
| | 25 | | 30 | | |
| *(Yang)* | | *(Yin)* | | | |

This way of counting the five elements is derived from an ancient chart called the *Ho-t'u*, or "River Chart." The *Ho-t'u* is a chart of the five elements as they exist in the Prior Heavens, that is, in their life-bearing order. Wood is said to give birth to fire, fire to earth, earth to metal, and metal to water. Water finally gives birth to wood, thus again starting the cycle. In this series, one finds the "*Chia*" or *Yang* aspect of wood joined with or "married" to the "*I*" or *Yin* aspect, which marriage brings forth life in wood.[4]

The *Ho-t'u* is thus made up of fifty-five dots, twenty-five of which represent the *Yang* elements, and thirty of which represent *Yin* elements. The elements are seen to be united, that is, the *Yin* and the *Yang* aspects of the five elements are "married" on the five points of the compass. The chart thus is symbolic of nature when life is being produced, and crops are growing.

An ancient legend tells how the mythical emperor of the east *Fu Hsi* discovered the chart on the back of a dragon-like horse which emerged from the Meng River (a tributary of the Yellow River in north China). *Fu Hsi* was inspired by the chart to draw the eight trigrams of the Prior Heavens.[5] The eight trigrams of *Fu Hsi* are not the popularly known eight trigrams of the *Book of Changes*, the *I-ching*. They do not symbolize change, but a state of continuing life and blessing. It is this chart which depicts the annual rebirth and renewal of the cosmos, an event celebrated at the winter solstice. One of the other names for this chart is the *Ling-pao* Five Talismans, which are planted into the village community during the village festival of renewal called *Chiao*.[6] In an esoteric sense, the chart symbolizes the activity of the transcendent *Tao*, called *Wu Wei*. According to the popular Taoist interpretation of *Wu Wei* (Transcendent Act), the term means essentially that primordial breath, spirit, and seminal essence, when preserved in the

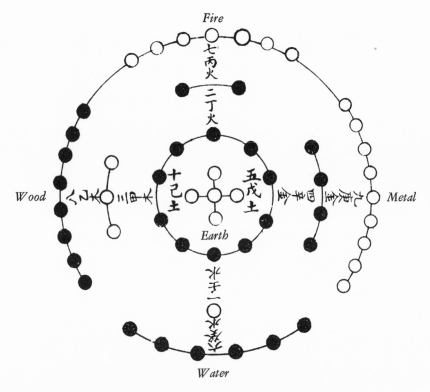

Figure 1. The *Ho-t'u*. Cf. *Ching Hua Lu Wen Tao-tzu Chiang Ching Hua Lu* (Taipei: Chen Shan Mei Press, 1966), p. 5.

center of the microcosm and the macrocosm, bring about eternal life and blessing. The state of the immanent *Tao*, on the other hand, defined as *Yu Wei*, is one where breath, spirit, and semen flow away, where *Yang* is gradually used and replaced by *Yin*, and the state of life yields to that of death and stillness as in winter. The chart called *Ho-t'u* depicts the *Yin* and *Yang* aspects of the five elements as joined in blissful marriage, thus causing eternal or constant life (*Ch'ang-sheng*).[7] It is the first step toward an alchemical refinement through meditation, whereby the elements wood and fire are joined to represent symbolically primordial breath and the primordial Heavenly Worthy; earth of center is taken to be spirit, symbolized by *Ling-pao* Heavenly Worthy; finally water and metal joined form seminal essence, *Tao-te* Heavenly Worthy.

圖之位方卦八羲伏

Figure 2. The eight trigrams of *Fu Hsi*. Taken from *Lai Chu I-ching T'u Chieh*, p. 23.

The process is known, in technical Taoist terms, as the joining of the "Three Fives." By referring to the *Ho-t'u*, it can readily be seen that wood is assigned the number 3, and fire the number 2. When joined, the equivalent is 5. Water is assigned the number 1, and metal the number 4; these two when joined again make 5. Finally, the *Wu* earth of center is assigned the number 5 of itself; the three fives are by euhemerism the Three Pure Ones, Primordial Heavenly Worthy, *Ling-pao* Heavenly Worthy, and *Tao-te* Heavenly Worthy. Their presence in the center of the microcosm means that the transcendent *Tao* of the Prior Heavens is present, thus

Figure 3. The *Lo-shu*. Taken from *Ching Hua Lu*, p. 7, and *I-Tao Hsin-fa*, p. 5.

bringing about *Ch'ang-sheng*, long life, continuing birth, and blessing. The *Ho-t'u* is, therefore, symbolic of the process of interior meditation which makes the life-bearing five elements present in the cosmos, and joins the "Three Fives," the three primordial spirits, in the center of the microcosm. The rituals of the *Chiao* festival demonstrate how Taoist liturgy can, in fact, be reduced to the cosmological principle of the *Ho-t'u*.[8]

But to accomplish the renewal of the universe, the *Ho-t'u* alone is not enough. The Taoist must also know the principles whereby change is caused in the universe, in order to reverse the process from *Yang* to *Yin*, and make *Yang* eternally on the pivot of life. In order to achieve this purpose, the Taoist makes use of a second chart called the *Lo-shu*. The *Lo-shu* is a chart of the Posterior Heavens of change. It was discovered by *Yü* the Great on the back of a tortoise which was seen emerging from the Lo River.[9]

Figure 4. The eight trigrams of King *Wen*. Taken from *Lai Chu I-ching T'u Chieh*, p. 24.

The obvious difference between the *Ho-t'u* and the *Lo-shu* is that the *Yin* and the *Yang* aspects of the five elements are no longer seen to be joined but are separated or divorced. The elements no longer bring life, but move inexorably away from *Yang* and blessing to *Yin* and death. *Yin* water is seen to overcome *Yang* fire (changed from the southern position in the *Ho-t'u* to west in the *Lo-shu*; fire is thus extinguished by the proximity of water in the west). *Yin* fire in the west then overcomes *Yang* metal in the south. *Yin* metal destroys wood in the east. Finally, *Yin* wood overcomes earth in the center. Looking more closely at the center of the *Lo-shu*, one sees that the ten central dots in the *Ho-t'u* are missing. The process of renewal cannot begin again. *Yin* is now supreme ruler, and *Yang* has been overcome. The cosmos must await the rebirth of *Yang* at the winter solstice, and the community of men must summon the Taoist to replant the *Ho-t'u* into the center of the universe, and cause nature to flourish again.

The *Lo-shu* is basically a diagram of change, and thus legend says that it was the inspiration for King *Wen* to create the *I-ching*, the *Book of Changes*.

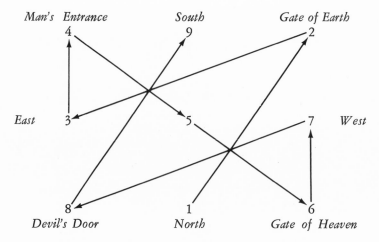

Figure 5. The *Lo-shu* used as the basis for ritual dance in Taoist liturgy.

It is basic to Taoist liturgy, the floor plan for the rituals of the *Chiao* festival being conceived of as taking place over a *Lo-shu*. The *T'an* area or sacred ritual area within the temple resembles the illustration above.[10]

The *Lo-shu* is thus the order of the eight trigrams used in the *Book of Changes*, as well as the floorplan for Taoist liturgy. *Yü* the Great was said to have divided the nine provinces of central China on the basis of the *Lo-shu*, and *Yao* with *Shun* created the model of the Chinese empire, as described in the *Hung Fan* chapter of the *Book of History*, on the same principle.[11] The *Lo-shu* is, furthermore, a magic square, that is, no matter in which direction the numbers are added, the sum will always be fifteen.[12]

One of the ritual dances performed by the Taoist, called the "Steps of *Yü*," which are thought to imitate the lame pace of *Yü* as he walked throughout the nine provinces stopping the floods and restoring the order and blessing of nature, is modeled on the *Lo-Shu*, from 1 through 9, arriving before the gods of the Prior Heavens, and ordering nature as *Yü* did in controlling the raging waters of the flood.

The *Lo-shu* is used in Taoist liturgy as the basic floor plan over which the liturgy is performed. The *Ho-t'u* is, in fact, interpreted to be the plan of the Prior Heavens, and a symbolic representation of the primordial breaths and heavenly spirits summoned during Taoist liturgy. With the help of the *Lo-shu* and the *Ho-t'u*, it is possible to provide an "emic" interpretation of the contents of the *Chiao* festival of cosmic renewal.

# IV

## The Chiao Ritual:
## An Emic Description

Attending a *Chiao* ritual is an experience that can be exhilarating or a lengthy ordeal of physical deprivation, depending upon the mood of the Taoists and their expertise. Although a *Chiao* can be performed at almost any time during the year, the highest frequency of occurrence in north Taiwan is from the end of the eleventh month through the first period of the twelfth month, before the winter solstice.[1] The weather is usually bright and clear, but it can be damp and rainy during the time of the performance, adding to the discomfort of sleeping on the concrete temple floor, with straw, a rush mat, and a quilt.

Once the purification has been performed (abstaining from marital relations and bathing in mugwort leaves, sulfur, and other cleansing elements), a participant is not supposed to leave the sacred area until the ritual is completed. All of the Taoist's physical needs are cared for in the temple— sleeping quarters and the Taoist's meditation room being on one side of the temple (preferably the east) and the kitchen and toilet facilities on the other. A guard stands at the door for twenty-four hours a day, refusing admittance to the unauthorized and protecting the ritually purified sacred area from contamination of any kind.

During the *Chiao* ceremony, from the night before entrance until the afternoon of the final day when the *P'u Tu* is performed, the eating of meat or any rich foods is forbidden. The fare usually consists of boiled rice, green vegetables, bamboo shoots, and bean curd. Fruits are placed on the various altars as offerings to the spirits, and the Taoists sometimes freely partake of these, as well as the bottles of wine (rice wine) used for the offerings, not in a sense of levity but as being the equal of the gods during the ritual ceremony.[2]

The people living in the temple during the ritual consist of the Taoist entourage, foreigners accompanying them as observers, the musicians, the kitchen crew, and the temple custodians, who are responsible for keeping the lamps filled with oil, the incense burning, and the bills paid. The leading members of the community, elected to be present from economic considerations as well as for leadership abilities, come and go as the ritual occasion demands. For the greater rituals, all are present, whereas for the lesser occasions, only those chosen to hold the incense burner or those who have sponsored that particular performance are present. On the wall nearest the entrance is posted a list of the village participants, and next to it a program of the various rituals and the approximate times for their commencement. Since the program and the wording of the texts are slightly different for the Red-head and the Black-head Taoists, a comparison of their respective rituals helps to identify the kind of Taoist and to give an over-all view of a complex set of liturgical performances (see Table 1).

A *Chiao* ritual such as is performed at village renewal festivals, or the dedication of a temple, may last for three, five, seven, or nine days, depending upon the financial state of the village and permission from the government, which does not wholly approve of such practices.[3] The usual period for a *Chiao* in present-day Taiwan is three days, and since this is the minimum length in which a more solemn *Su Ch'i* ritual may be performed, the program for a three-day *Chiao* will be listed in synoptic form; one of the schedules from the *Tao Tsang*, volume 209, will be compared with the Black-head and the Red-head versions.

In the following lists, several things are to be noted. The first is that the Sung dynasty canonical lists of the rituals are not complete, a fact noted by the Taiwan Taoists who have access to the Taipei reprints of the *Tao Tsang*, the printed form of the Taoist canon. The Taoists' own versions, passed down from father to son for many generations, are not only more complete, but make the canonical texts almost unintelligible without reference to them.[4] A second observation is that many of the rituals are popular in nature, meant either for the public to witness, or else to be done in the "*Wai T'an*" or the southern section of the sacred temple area. Thus the *Fa Piao* announcing ceremony is done to the south, the Taoist going outside the sacred temple area to perform in public. In more pious communities most of the village will be awake at midnight to witness this event, while in other *Chiao* rituals it is witnessed only by the village elders and the Taoist entourage, beginning after midnight, and not ending until two or three in the morning.

There are, then, basically three kinds of rituals in the *Chiao* ceremonies. There are, first, the orthodox rituals of the Heavenly Master sect of Taoism, which require an ordained Taoist of a sixth rank[5] or above to perform; when performing such rituals the Taoist wears the solemn red robes and gold crown, with the flame pin inserted in the top. Second, there are the canons, read for merit and repentance, which any member of the Taoist entourage may chant, and which besides providing merit for living and dead, fill in the many hours with chanting not unlike the performances in Buddhist temples. Finally, there are the highly dramatic pieces, done in a tunic or a smaller green and red robe with the gold crown, but without the flame pin; these are a sort of ritual catechetics, teaching Taoist ideas through a highly instructive dramatic form for the edification of the entire village populace. Such ritual is sometimes performed inside the temple in the section entitled "outer" *T'an*, and is sometimes performed in the plaza directly in front of the temple. Thus, a ritual such as the *Fa Piao*, "Announcing to the Spirits," is partially done inside the temple, facing the south, and is partially performed outside, so that all may see.

## The First Day

The very first duty to be attended to is the setting up of the sacred *T'an* area, the turning of the village temple into a Taoist "*T'an*" altar, representing the cosmos. The original *T'an* structures were square, built in the open, according to the diagrams of the *Tao Tsang*.[6] They were composed of three squares superimposed on each other, the "outer" being the largest, then the "center," and finally the "inner" area. Present-day *T'an* areas are rectangular projections of the former, built on the same principle.

The "*T'an*" is a representation of the cosmos, both the macrocosm and the microcosm, the center being the "Yellow Court" residence of the "*Tao*." The "Posterior Heavens" drawing of the eight trigrams of King *Wen* is figuratively represented in the central area.

The Taoists set up the temple as illustrated in Figure 3, hanging scrolls to represent the spirits indicated, and putting all the movable gods of the temple and visiting deities in the south, in the place of worship. The musicians sit on the west side, in the outer area, and the observer just beneath the tiger scroll. The laymen of the community kneel or stand in the center of the outer area.

In the north of the *T'an* area are hung the scrolls of the Three Pure Ones, *Yüan-shih* Heavenly Worthy, *Ling-pao* Heavenly Worthy, and *Tao-te* Heavenly Worthy or *Lao-tzu*. To their left, that is, on the east side of the north wall, is the pavilion of the Jade Emperor, and on the west side, the pavilion of *Ts'z-wei Ta-ti*, the Great Emperor of the Purple Palace of the North. The east wall of the temple houses all the spirit bureaus of heaven

Table 1. Order for a Three-Day *Chiao*

| TT 209, Ch. II: *Chiao* for dedicating a building (Sung) | Black-head *Chiao* | Red-head *Chiao* |
|---|---|---|
| | *First Day* | |
| 1. Setting up the *T'an* altar | 1. Setting up the *T'an* altar | 1. Setting up the *T'an* alter |
| 2. Inviting the spirits | 2. Announcing to the spirits (south)* | 2. Announcing to the spirits (south)* |
| 3. Summoning the spirits | 3. Inviting the spirits (north) | 3. Inviting the spirits (north) |
| 4. Jade Emperor canon | 4. Purifying the sacred area (*Chin T'an*) | 4. Sending off the gods of soil and hearth* |
| 5. Purifying the sacred area (*Chin T'an*) | 5. Jade Pivot canon | 5. Three Officials canon |
| 6. (Night) *Fen Teng* | 6. Noon offering | 6. North Pole canon |
| 7. *Su Ch'i*, planting the five true writs | 7. Canons of repentance | 7. South Star canon |
| | 8. *Fen Teng* (night) (new light); sounding bell and chime | 8. Noon offering |
| | 9. (Midnight) *Su Ch'i*, planting the five true writs | 9. Three Origins canon |
| | | 10. *Fen Teng* (night) (new light only) |
| | *Second Day* | |
| 1. Morning Audience | 1. Re-invite | 1. Re-invite |
| 2. Noon Audience | 2. Morning Audience (green) | 2. Morning Audience |
| 3. (Noon) offerings and petitions | 3. Noon Audience (yellow) | 3. Noon Audience, with part of the *Fen Teng*, and ritual dance steps of the twenty-eight constellations |
| 4. Night Audience | 4. Noon offering | 4. Noon offering |
| | 5. Canons of repentance (and *Tu Jen Ching*) | 5. Canons of repentance (the *Tu Jen Ching*) |
| | 6. Night Audience (white) | 6. Night Audience |
| | 7. Floating the 10,000 lanterns* | 7. Floating the 10,000 lanterns* |
| | | 8. *Chin T'an*. Purifying the sacred area (*Su Ch'i* missing) |

Third Day

| | | |
|---|---|---|
| 1. Canonical texts | 1. Re-invite | 1. Re-invite |
| 2. Closing the T'an area | 2. Invitation to "T'ien Kung"* | 2. Invitation to "T'ien Kung"* |
| 3. Sending off the petitions | 3. Jade Emperor canon | 3. Jade Emperor canon |
| 4. Offering food to the souls | 4. Tao Ch'ang; closing the T'an area by collecting the five writs | 4. Noon offering |
| 5. Seeing off the spirits | 5. Sending off the petitions; "Chin Piao"* | 5. Offering the petitions* |
| | 6. Noon offering | 6. Su Ch'ao, or Ju Ch'ao (Tao Ch'ang) |
| | 7. P'u Tu; feeding the hungry souls* | 7. Closing the T'an |
| | 8. Thanking the spirits | 8. P'u Tu; feeding the hungry spirits* |
| | 9. Seeing off the spirits* | 9. Thanking the spirits |
| | | 10. Seeing off the spirits* |

* Indicates popular ritual, performed in the open or exterior area for the whole populace to see. The Jade Emperor canon and invitation to T'ien Kung is performed in the exterior T'an. The P'u Tu is done in the open plaza before the temple. (T'ien Kung is the popular name for the Jade Emperor.)

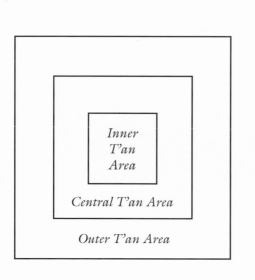

Figure 1.  Older *T'an*.

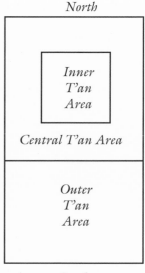

Figure 2.  Present-day T'an.

and earth and the dragon spirit *K'ang Yuan-shuai*. The west wall supports the scrolls of the water and mountain bureaus of spirits, and the spirit-general of the west, *Chao Yüan-shuai*. Finally in the outer *T'an* area are the assembled local deities, the *Ch'eng Huang*, gods of the soil, *Ma-tsu*, the goddess of the sea, and other popular *Shen-ming*, "Bright Spirits" of the folk religion. They, with the people of the community, are now in the position of onlookers, whilst the Taoists and the spirits of the heavens have that highest of all experiences, the encounter with the *Tao*, which renews village life and frees the orphan souls from their life of wandering in the underworld. For the orphan souls too have their place at the *Chiao* ritual, and will be summoned by the floating of lanterns on the evening of the second day to attend the great banquet on the afternoon of the third day. The *Chiao* is now ready to begin.

### 1.  Fa Piao:  Announcing to the Spirits

The *Fao Piao* ceremony takes place at midnight, and is an exterior-oriented rite, facing the south. The Taoist summons all the spirits of the three worlds—heaven, earth, and water regions—to attend the *Chiao*. The ceremony is performed by the Red-head Taoists in a seven-word popular verse which parallels the orthodox Black-head Taoist version in five-character classical verse. In its orthodox form, the ceremony is similar to the *Chin Piao*, or sending of the petition on the third day of the *Chiao*. The ceremony ends with the sending or burning of an official document, the *Piao*, declaring the purpose of the *Chiao*, the people's names who are participating, and the *Chiao* program. The burning is done in a great cauldron in front of the temple, and includes also paper horses, passports and a host of other talismans and documents.

The ceremony is accompanied by a Red-head ritual of "Opening the Eyes," that is, making present the spirits of the three worlds by touching a brush dipped in blood to the scrolls and statues of the spirits within and without the *T'an* area. The brush must be dipped in the blood of a cock's comb, a duck's bill, and the tongue of the Taoist, which has been slightly scratched with the great sword he carries. The rite is frenzied and

Figure 3. The Taoist envisions the eight trigrams of King *Wen* (the *Lo-shu*) on the temple floor during ritual.

mediumistic in nature, and shows the difference of origin of the Red-head and the more stately orthodox Black-head. A Taoist who performs this rite shows himself to have been originally either a *Shen-hsiao* sixth-order Taoist, or a heterodox Taoist who has purchased his way into orthodox ranks. The Red-head liturgy being far more colorful, it, of course, lends itself to being watched and appreciated at village festivals, and, therefore, many of the Black-heads are forced to perform this kind of ritual for economic considerations.

### 2. *Ch'ing Shen: Inviting the Spirits*

The *Ch'ing Shen* ceremony takes place facing the north, in the central *T'an* area, and the Taoist wears his great robes and gold crown. The ceremony can take place immediately after the *Fa Piao*, that is, early in the morning of the first day. One by one, 280 or 360 spirits are invited to be present for the *Chiao*, and a great document called a *Tieh*, an official dispatch, is sent to heaven to accomplish the invitation.

Early in the morning of the first day occurs a ceremony called the "Raising of the Standards." Throughout most of Taiwan, three extremely high bamboo poles are set up on a platform in front of the temple. These three poles bear a standard and a lantern at the base; the first is dedicated to the Jade Emperor and the Heavenly Spirits; the second is dedicated to the North Pole constellation, the Big Dipper and its seven star spirits; the third is the lantern and standard of the orphan souls, to be summoned for the banquet on the third day.[7] The standards are raised in a brief ceremony on this first morning and serve as a warning to spirits and mortals that the *Chiao* ceremony is now going on within the temple.

### 3. *Chin T'an: Purifying the Sacred T'an Area*

The dramatic *Chin T'an* ceremony is one of the best documented in the *Tao Tsang*. The texts extant in Taiwan are almost identical with the printed canonical versions, and the version used by the Taoist *Chuang-ch'en* follows the rubrics to be found in the *Tao Tsang*, volume 985, chapter 7. The work was compiled by the Sung dynasty Taoist *Lü T'ai-ku*, from earlier sources including the T'ang dynasty Taoist *Tu Kuang-t'ing*.[8]

By many of the Taiwanese Taoists the *Chin T'an* ritual of purification is performed out of its proper place, on the evening of the second day; some of the Red-head Taoists perform it immediately preceding the *Su-Ch'ao* or *Tao Ch'ang* on the third day. *Chuang* continually inveighs against this practice and places it in proper order on the first day.

The Taoist chosen to perform the *Chin T'an* ritual dresses in the robes of a *Tu Chiang*, that is a chief cantor, with the shorter green and red tunic, the black cap and gold crown. The flame pin is not inserted. The *Tu Chiang* is the personification of the principle *Yang*; he usually stands at the left of the central altar, the *Yang* position, and, therefore, in the Red-head liturgy he is called the "Dragon." Since it is his role to perform this rite, he enters from the earth gate, the *K'un* position in the southwest, whereas the high priest, the *Kao-kung Fa-shih*, enters from the gate of heaven in the northwest, when he initiates ritual ceremony.

From his position at the entrance of earth, the Taoist priest must "*ts'un*" or fix in his mind the images of the spirits who will be summoned to assist him. He first sees in detail the three spirits in the handle of the constellation of Ursa Major, the "Heavenly Realized Lords *T'ang, Ko, and Chou*," each with his own special apparel. He sees them entering the *T'an* area, swords in hand, ready to assist at the purification.[9] Then he envisions directly above his head all seven stars of the Big Dipper, and in the four directions around him, the four mythical creatures: Green Dragon to the east, Red Phoenix to the south, White Tiger to the west, and the Armored Tortoise in the north. Now above him appear sun, moon, and the five planets.

He next must summon the spirits, by putting his thumb on the middle joint of the middle finger of the left hand, and the fourth finger in the center of the palm, a sacred sacramental "*Mudra*," efficacious for summoning the deities he has envisioned. Thereupon he invites the Green Dragon from the left, thinking of the corresponding constellations of the east.[10] Accompanied by a great thundering noise, graphically represented by thundering drums and cymbals of the musicians, the dragon arrives. The Taoist envisions the dragon spewing great clouds of green smoke, which fill the *T'an* area with vapor. Next, he calls from the west the White Tiger, from its corresponding western constellation, and again the tiger responds with a roar, coming in a cloud of white vapor. The Red Bird of the south is summoned, with a host of spirits, in clouds of jade color. With him come the spirits of the five colors, and the six symbols, inhabitants of the microcosm. Finally, out of the north comes the mysterious dark creature, all armored, in the form of a turtle-serpent, born by transformation from the great *Yin*. The creature of the north is accompanied by a host of spirits that are efficacious for expelling evil and are enveloped in a dark vapor.[11]

Fortified by this splendid force of formidable deities, the priest then closes both hands in a *Mudra* where all the fingers of both hands and the thumb touch the center of the palm, thus summoning all the spirits, the sun and the moon, the four directions or seasons, the nine provinces, all sixteen generals subordinate to the *T'ai-yi* deity in the east, and finally the spirit officials of heaven, earth, and the underworld.

The Taoist priest then takes the great sword in his right hand and recalls in an incantation that the sword was forged from the five elements, fire, wood, water, earth, and metal. Hardened into matchless steel, it is a sword for killing or forbidding entrance to evil spirits and demons. It is this great sword which helps the *Tao* to be taught and spread abroad everywhere throughout the world. The twenty-eight constellations and the seven stars of the Dipper all support its holder and spread the hundred blessings to the thousand directions of the cosmos.[12]

In his left hand the priest takes the small metal bowl, filled with water, and says that it is not common water taken from the rivers, streams, or oceans; it is spiritual water, emitted by a dragon, for purifying heaven and earth. For the ruler who drinks it, there will be life for ten thousand years; today it will be used to purify and expel sullied demon breath.[13]

The Taoist then commands the five dragons of the five directions, by means of talismans written in the air with the sword, to enter the purified water, with the pure primordial breath from the five directions, and the five stars. It is through the use of this sword, "no ordinary sword" the text says, that the talismans can be written and the water purified, "now no longer ordinary water,"[14] for the breath of the five directions has now penetrated it. Taking a sip from the bowl, he finishes the incantation with a crescendo command, and blows a huge spray of water, like a cloud of vapor, from his mouth.

Thereupon, he proceeds to each of the intermediate directions, the devil's door, heaven's gate, man's entrance, and the door to earth, purifying them with the great sword, and a cloud of vapor blown from the mouth. A second time around, he "fixes" the spirit-generals of the northeast and the northwest, asking them for special protection of village and nation, keeping even the smallest demons from entrance.

Having summoned the spirit-generals of the north for military aid in the war against evil, the Taoist then paces to the earth entrance in the southeast, where he summons the emperors of the five directions, according to the formula of the *Ho-t'u*, with a symbolic number assigned to each spirit.[15]

Respectfully on high we invite
The Green Emperor of the East,
Wood official who dissolves impurities;
Lord messengers, nine men.
The Red Emperor of the South,
Fire official, dissolve of impurities;
Lord messengers, three men.
The White Emperor of the West,
Metal official, dissolver of impurities;

Lord messengers, seven men.
Black Emperor of the North,
Water official, dissolver of impurities;
Lord messengers, five men.
Yellow Emperor of the Center,
Earth official, dissolver of impurities;
Lord messengers, twelve men.
Ye who bear on high the talisman
That dissolves impurities, Lord messengers;
Ye who carry below the talisman
That dissolves impurities, Lord messengers;
Ye who this year, this month,
This day, this moment bear the talismans
To dissolve impurities, messenger troops,
Young men, Jade girls, 120 in all,
Altogether, come down to this sacred *T'an!*[16]

Having finished the first circumvolution, the Taoist then paces in ritual step to the west, and faces the east. He fixes within himself the Emperor of the East, and the green primordial breath of spring. Then from the west he paces to the north, from which position he faces the south, and again, "*ts'un*," fixes within himself, the Red Emperor of the South, with his three young men and the red cinnabar breath of summer. The Taoist sees the Red Phoenix spitting forth fire, a fire which melts rocks and metal; an imagery full of symbolic meaning for the purification of evil spirits. Thereupon, pacing to the east, he faces west, and brings within himself the White Emperor of the West with seven men and the white vapor of autumn. He prays that the Western Emperor's retainers dispel and obliterate harmful vapors, and settle the "*P'o*" or *Yin* aspect of the soul. He then moves to the southern position where he faces north, calling the Black Emperor of the North, the "five" primordial breaths, with an imagery of somber black dragons belching forth lightning, destroying the legions of demonic soldiers, protecting the village families, and bringing peace to the nation.

Finally, he steps to the center, where he fixes within himself the Yellow Emperor of the Center, the "*Hun-t'un* Primordial One Yellow Breath,"[17] changing old age into youth, so that at the reading and sending off of the *fu*-talisman (of the north), all living things may with great joy "enter the *Tao* of the *Wu Wei*."[18] The "sending off of the talisman" thus symbolizes a contractual treaty with the spirits of the Prior Heavens. The treaty will be signed and ratified during the coming ritual acts of the *Chiao* festival.

Turning to the people of the community and the Taoist entourage, the priest proceeds to purify them. The first reads an incantation over the water, and blows the purifying liquid on the people present. "Water," says the Taoist, "has no fixed form; but by means of the incantation its form is now fixed. It is, here in my hands, now named spirit water; sprayed on the heavens above, it purifies; sprayed on the earth below, it causes eternal peace; spewed on man, it produces eternal life; blown on demons, it causes their form to be destroyed. With one spray, one becomes as pure as dew; with the second spray, clean as fresh-fallen snow; the third puff, and the 10,000 evil forces are cut off, demons are entirely suppressed, and natural calamities are brought to an end. Then from the South Pole Star will come a fire of life, a longevity which matches that of the sun and the moon."[19]

The chief Taoist and all present are then purified by the reciting of prayers that penetrate deeply into every part of the body. The Taoist purifies the five organs and their spirits, the six intestines, the seven ruling officials, the nine palaces of the head, the twelve spirit rooms, the 180 spirit passes, 360 bones and joints, 1,200 qualitative forms, and 12,000 seminal sparks of light in the bodies of all that are present. It is interesting that in spite of minor textual differences, the texts of *Chuang* and the Sung dynasty *Tao Tsang* version of *Lü T'ai-ku* coincide here, with the same wording. The three "*Hun*" (*Yang*) souls on the left, and the seven "*P'o*" (*Yin*) souls on the right are each to be filled and made one with *Tao*. Through the purificatory cleansing of the ritual, all three of the microcosmic sections of the body, with eight orders of spirits in each, corresponding to the three times eight or twenty-four cosmic realms, are filled with the *Tao*. "Now," says the Taoist, "I am the child of *T'ai Shang*, the Great Ultimate, the grandchild of the mysterious ruler (the *Tao*)."

Above, my head is crowned with the Vermillion Phoenix,
Beneath, my feet supported by the Dark Warrior;
On the left, the Imperial Green Dragon,
On my right crouches the White Tiger.[20]

The texts of the heterodox Red-head Taoists here differ from the Sung dynasty text of *Lü T'ai-ku*, in that the Dragon goes ahead in a welcoming gesture, while the Tiger falls in behind, beating gong and drum. The Sung dynasty text, as well as the text of *Chuang*, is longer, with Dragon welcoming, Phoenix with flags, Tiger following from behind, and the Dark Warrior with drum and gongs. Altogether they purify the body of the head Taoist and the entourage, hinting for the first time at the climax of the ritual, the sealing of the sacred area from the evil influence of *Yin*.

The classical texts of *Chuang* and the Sung dynasty version then quote the *Huang T'ing Ching*, an incantation to the corresponding spirits of the five organs, naming them with their functions:[21]

| 1. The heart spirit | Cinnabar origin | Lord who guards the soul |
| 2. Lung spirit | Bright flowery | Lord of void fulfillment |
| 3. Liver spirit | Dragon vapor | Lord of cherished brightness |
| 4. Kidney spirit | Mysterious brightness | Lord who nourishes the infant |
| 5. Spleen spirit | Eternal presence | Lord of the abode of spirit |

The incantation ends with a plea to keep seminal essence always within the heart, preserved within, rather than flowing out; the text hopes to preserve eternally the presence of the five spirits of the center, the six spirits of the lower body, the twelve realized men. All are to be "*ts'un*," fixed within the heart, day and night, whereby eternal life will be gained.

A second incantation follows, also from the *Yellow Court Canon*, naming the spirits of the upper part of the body, the hair, the brain, the eyes, the nose, the tongue, the teeth, the thousand spirits of the head and face. The spirits are purified and warned to preserve the *Yang* aspects of the soul, the "*Hun*," and to nullify the *Yin* aspects of the soul, the "*P'o*."[22]

The Taoist then calls upon the orthodox spirits of the seven Pole Stars to come and fill the body; he asks specifically that the three Pole Stars of the Dipper's handle, which control man's destiny, come and fill the three realms of the body, upper, middle and lower, in order to give birth to, nourish, and protect the "*Tao*-life" conceived within. It is specifically into the Taoist's body that the spirits are called; and with the Taoist as mediator, they are infused into the bodies of all those present.

Next the Taoist performs a sacred dance called the "Steps of *Yü*," based upon the nine positions of the magic square called *Lo Shu*, dragging one foot behind the other, imitating the lame pace of *Yü* when he stopped the floods, wearied by endless meritorious wanderings. The steps represent the magic square of nine numbers, which, no matter how they are added, always come out to be fifteen, the six of earth and the nine of heaven in harmony. The "Steps of *Yü*" are traced around the eight positions of the trigrams plus the center, with the same efficacy that *Yü* the Great had when he paced around the nine provinces of the ancient empire, ordering nature and stopping natural calamity.

As he performs the steps, the Taoist again purifies the four directions by blowing sprays of purified water from his mouth, standing first in the northeast, the Devil's Gate, and purifying the east; then from the southwest, the Door of Man, he purifies the west; finally from the northwest, the Gate of Heaven, he purifies the north, asking each time that the true, realized *Tao*-breath be implanted in the sacred area. Then, he steps to the center, and facing the northwest, the Gate of Heaven, begs that the "realized breath of the center" come down into the sacred *T'an* area.[23]

Now the climax has been reached, as the Taoist begins to trace another heavenly dance step, that of the seven stars of the Great Dipper, in the center of the area. He summons the exorcising spirits of the north to close all entrance to the sacred area from spirits of malevolence, *Yin*, or death. Next, he summons all the heavenly spirits, warriors on horseback, all the earthly spirits, immortal soldiers with their mounts, all of the realized men with their armies and steeds, the sun and the moon and the stars of the heavens, the nine heavenly officials and the emperors of the five directions, the Three Great Rivers and the Four Great Oceans, the Five Peaks, all the hosts of mounted spirit-soldiers, inviting each with fierce and awesome demeanor to assemble now at once in the sacred area, right at the devil's door, and seal it forever.

Taking the great sword in his right hand,[24] the Taoist then draws a circle on the floor, three revolutions from left to right, that is, clockwise, going toward the center. Then over this he draws another circle, this time from right to left, counterclockwise. Over these two concentric circles he then draws seven horizontal lines, representing heaven, and seven vertical lines, representing earth. By thus sealing the Gate of Hell, that is, the northeast position, the primordial breath of earth and the seminal essence of wood can no longer flow away, but they with the *Tao* (spirit) can now be kept within, that is, in the Yellow Court of the center. Finally, he draws the character for demon, "*Kuei*," in the center of the figure, and runs it through with the sword, spraying the purifying water on it from his mouth. The Gate of Demons is now sealed, with primordial breath, semen, and spirit kept within, and the evil influences of *Yin* locked without. The sacred *T'an* area having been purified, the members of the entourage are filled with the orthodox *Yang* spirit of the heavens, the five elements are now in their life-giving order bearing "*Yang*," and the liturgy of the encounter with the spirits of the Prior Heavens may begin.[25]

Since only the most orthodox of Taoists place this ritual in its proper order, it is usually to be found either in the early evening of the second day, or even is performed as late as the third day, by the popular Taoists of the *Shen-hsiao* or lowest sixth grade of Taoist priesthood. The ritual, whenever performed, is surely one of the most colorful and pleasant to watch, and requires great agility and perfection on the part of the Taoist who performs it.

### 4.   *The Canons of Merit and Repentance*

The first morning and afternoon of the *Chiao* festival are filled with the reading of the canons of merit and repentance, including the canons of the

Three Officials, the North Pole Star, the Southern Star, the canons of the Three Origins, and especially the canon of the Jade Pivot. The last mentioned of these texts is considered by Taoists to be the most esoteric, whereas the canons of the Three Officials, the North Pole star, and so forth are used by adherents of the popular religion and by Buddhist monasteries as well. The canons may be bought in the bookshops and are chanted in the rituals of Buddhist monasteries for public festivals.[26]

## 5.   *The Noon Offering*

The stately Noon Offering ritual takes place at noon on all three days of the *Chiao* ceremony. It consists of offering incense, flowers, lighted candles, tea, wine, fruit, rice, steamed bread, and gold. It is accompanied by dance and hymns and requires great skill and finesse to perform.[27] Each of the nine items is offered to the gods by a stately ritual dance.

The afternoon continues with the readings of the canons of repentance, the Upper, Middle, and Lower Origin canons, popular rituals for public perusal, including the planting of small paper and food effigies of the spirits of the five directions around the village, and other dramatized versions of the purification of the temple, such as expelling of the spirits that bring calamities. The devout laymen often schedule so many of these popular rituals for the Taoist to perform that time does not permit all to be done. A discreet bargaining by the Taoist removes some of the onus and allows short intervals for rest in the almost continual twenty-four-hour-a-day liturgical performances.

## 6.   *The Fen Teng: Lighting of the New Fire*

The evening of the first day is the climax of the initial day's ritual. The first ritual act is the famous *Fen Teng*, or lighting of all the lamps of the temple with a new fire kindled with the "flames of the sun," or pure *Yang*. The ritual is, in effect, a reading of the forty-second chapter of the *Lao-tzu*, describing the protogenesis of the myriad creatures.

A new fire is lit outside the *T'an* area by striking a match. Two torches dipped in lamp oil are lighted with the new fire, and brought into the sacred *T'an* area. The action symbolizes taking fire from the "Great *Yang*," the sun, and relighting the lamps of the temple. Thus the light of new *Yang* is seen to renew the darkness of the world of *Yin*, making the night seem as day, and lighting the temple votive lamps with a new, life-bringing fire. The ritual is always performed in the darkness of evening; as the new fire is carried into the temple, each of the Taoists lights a taper, which is carried throughout the ritual dances of the *Fen Teng* ceremony. The high priest begins the rite with the following words:[28]

The Void Transcendent Mysterious *Tao*,
In the beginning gave birth to the One.
The One, it is primordial breath's beginning!
Therefore let us light one lamp before *Yüan-shih* [Heavenly Worthy]
To illumine the first green ancestral primordial breath's
Coming forth!

When the high priest finishes the chant, the chief cantor or *Tu-chiang* then lights the lamp, which is in front of the scroll to the *Yüan-shih* Heavenly Worthy, and the entire Taoist entourage sings a lengthy hymn in praise.

Next the high priest intones:

The Tao gave birth to the One Breath,
The One gave birth to the Two;

The Two, it is the second of the Primordial Breaths;
Therefore let us light a second lamp
In front of the Primordial Emperor [*Ling-pao* Heavenly Worthy],
Thereby illuminating the beginning of the
*Shih-huan* "Two" primordial breath.

The assistant cantor, the *Fu-chiang*, then lights the lamp in front of the scroll to the *Ling-pao* Heavenly Worthy, and all sing a very long hymn in his honor.

Thirdly, the high priest intones:

The One gives birth to the Two;
The Two gives birth to the Three;
The Three, it is next in the "series" of Primordial breaths;
Therefore let us in third place light a lamp
In front of the Primordial "Old" One [*Lao-tzu*]
Thereby illuminating Primordial Old-One's coming forth.

The *Tu-chiang* then lights the lamp in front of the scroll to the *Tao-te* Heavenly Worthy, *Lao-tzu*, and again a lengthy hymn is sung in his honor. Finally, the high priest sings the complete text of the forty-second chapter of the *Lao-tzu*, "The *Tao* gives birth to the One, the One gives birth to the Two, and the Two gives birth to the Three; the Three gives birth to the myriad creatures."[29] Whereupon the community elders, five in number, step forward and offer five gifts: a tray with fruits, representing wood of the east, and asking for fertility of the five grains; a tray with gold coins, representing metal of the west, begging for prosperity; a plate with a fish on it, representing water of the north, and the fecundity which it brings to man and the world around him; a tray with ashes, representing fire of the south, begging that each home be filled with blessings; and the metal bowl of the

Taoists, now emptied of its water, representing the earth, the center from which all blessings come.[30] The Taoist prays that all four seasons be free from catastrophe, and filled with blessing. Thereupon, all the lamps in the temple are lit, and indeed night becomes as day, the light of new *Yang* symbolically filling the sacred area.

Two more ceremonies, appended to the *Fen Teng* ceremony, may be added at this time. The first is called "Rolling up the Screen," recalling the Imperial Audience, in which a screen is imagined to be in the center of the "Inner *T'an*" area, representing the place where the audience with the *Tao* is to take place. The screen is "rolled up" by symbolic gesture, making the first of the Three Pure Ones, *Yüan-shih* Heavenly Worthy, present in the center. Then the screen is rolled up a second time, and the *Ling-pao* Heavenly Worthy is present in the center. Finally, it is rolled up a third time, and the *Tao-te* Heavenly Worthy is present. With the three Heavenly Worthies present, the audience with the *Tao*, which purifies and brings longevity, is soon to begin. The ritual, when placed after the *Fen Teng*, is perhaps out of place, and certain passages in the Taoist canon indicate that it should be performed before the triple audiences with the *Tao* on the following day. The Red-head *Shen-hsiao* Taoists of Hsinchu, T'ao-yuan, and Taipei counties perform it during the Noon Audience on the second day. It is to be found in the *Tao Tsang* separate from the *Fen Teng* ceremony. In a version found by the author in the British Museum, taken from the Taoist *Ch'en Hsiang-yü* of Chang-chou in the 1820's, it is written in as a part of the *Fen Teng* ceremony, and is performed that way in many parts of Taiwan today.[31]

A second ceremony that is sometimes performed after the *Fen Teng* on the first evening of the *Chiao* is the "Sounding the Bell and Chime." This ceremony consists in sounding first the metal bowl, placed on the right side of the table in the center of the area, in front of the chief cantor (the *Tu-chiang*), twenty-four times, representing the influence of *Yang* throughout the cosmos. Next the wooden fish, on the left side of the table, in front of the assistant cantor (*Fu-chiang*), is sounded twenty-four times, representing the powers of *Yin*. Then both are sounded together thirty-six times, symbolizing the harmonious union of *Yin* and *Yang* that gave birth to the myriad things. Finally, the metal gong is struck nine times, the number of "old" *Yang*, and the wooden fish is sounded six times, the number of "old" *Yin*, the breaths of heaven and earth after the consummation of the union. This quiet and lovely ritual is performed during the Noon Audience by the Red-head Taoists of north Taiwan. It is to be found in a separate place from the *Fen Teng* ritual in the Taoist canon, and is performed by most of the

Black-head Taoists immediately after the *Fen Teng* ceremony during the evening of the first day.[32]

### 7.   *The Su Ch'i.   The Ling-pao Five Talismans*

The *Su Ch'i* is no doubt one of the oldest and by far the most secret and esoteric of the *Chiao* rituals.  The *Su Ch'i* in its present form can be found in the Taoist canon with the signature of the fifth-century Taoist master *Lu Hsiu-ching*.[33]  The term itself means "Night Announcement," a name which deliberately obscures the significance of the rite.  The core of the *Su Ch'i* is planting of the *Ling-pao* Five Talismans, and the reading of the *Ling-pao* "True Writs," in words similar to those found in the passage from the *Huai-nan-tzu*, as well as to the *Yüeh Ling* chapter of the *Book of Rites*.  The term *Su Ch'i*, however, is used by the Taoists of Taiwan to designate any liturgical performance which lasts more than twenty-four hours, that is, which carries through one day into the next.  The field-worker or acquaintance of a Taoist in Taiwan, therefore, who hears that a *Su Ch'i* is going to be performed, will be disappointed when the rituals turn out no different from the daily order of rituals performed for a god's festival in the local temple.  A solemn *Su Ch'i* rite is technically only supposed to be performed in a *Chiao* festival which lasts longer than three days; it is essential to the ritual that it be followed by the Three Audiences, and then by the "Audience with the *Tao* in the Center," which goes by the name *Tao Ch'ang*, on the last day of the festival.  The reasons for this necessary progression of rituals will become clear.  The Taoist, in fact, appears to be alchemically purifying the microcosm, through a series of meditations, for the indwelling of the eternal transcendent *Tao*.  The *Su Ch'i* is the first step of the process.

The *Su Ch'i* is, therefore, the application of the *Ling-pao* Five Talismans, a form of *Ho-t'u*, to the cosmos.  The spirits summoned by the Taoist into the village temple, and into the bodies of the people present, are personifications of the principles delineated under the title *Ho-t'u*, the magical chart which renews the cosmos.  The manner of performing the ritual differs in externals from area to area, but the internal meditation going on within the Taoist's mind is essentially one.  When the emperor is present to witness a *Su Ch'i*, the Taoist canon relates, nine bolts of green silk are to be put on a table to the east of the sacred *T'an* area; three bolts of red silk are placed on a table to the south.  Seven bolts of white silk are in the west, five in the north, and one bolt of pure yellow-gold silk is placed in the center.  Some Taoists use twenty-five acolytes, five dressed in each of the five colors, green, red, white, black, and yellow, standing in the respective directions of the compass.  Others use five bushels of rice, representing the five sacred peaks, located in the five directions. Other Taoists again simply meditate, while the members of the entourage chant the liturgy and describe what is happening in the high priest's mind.

The Taoist entourage enters the sacred *T'an* area in solemn procession. The ritual begins, as do all orthodox liturgies, with a meditative hymn, the dispatching of an official document of petition, and the construction of the "*mandala*" in the mind of the high priest, wherein he envisions the gods of the Prior Heavens filling the sacred *T'an* area. The nucleus of the *Su Ch'i* ritual then begins.

The high priest sees a green vapor coming from his liver; corresponding to the green vapor, he imagines the mythical emperor of the eastern heavens, *Fu Hsi*, coming with his retainers, 90,000 in number. There are the spirits of the eastern heavens, the spirit of Jupiter, the *Sui* star, the spirit of the eastern peak, and the gods of the eastern ocean. The chief cantor intones:

Let the High Priest Implant the True Writ of the East.

The *Ling-pao* talisman of the east is burned, the *Ling* part of the contract ascending to the heavens, the *Pao* or life-giving vapor of the element wood, with the myriad spirits of the east, filling the body of the Taoist and all present. In a symbolic gesture, the *Ling-pao* True Writ can be pressed down in the bushel of rice which represents the eastern peak, but in fact the "pressing down" or insertion of the *Pao* half of the talisman is done by the interior meditation of the high priest. The element wood of the *Ho-t'u*, that is, the *Yang* and *Yin* aspect of wood in harmonious union, has been received as a precious *Pao* treasure into the microcosm of the community. The entourage then proceeds to the south, and the same process continues in the mind of the Taoist. The god of the south, *Shen Nung*, with his 30,000 retainers, arrives, enveloped in red vapor. The chief cantor intones:

Let the High Priest Implant the True Writ of the South.

The *Ling-pao* talisman of the south is burned, and the true writ is planted in the bushel of rice. Through the efficacious meditation of the Taoist, the productive life-giving element fire of the *Ho-t'u* is implanted in the hearts of all present.

The rite continues through the five directions, with the *Ling-pao* talisman being burned in each of the directions, and the Taoist by his meditation implanting the life-giving vapors of metal in the lungs, water in the kidneys, and earth in the spleen. The colors of the vapor are subsequently white, black, and yellow, respectively. The god of the west comes with

70,000 retainers, the god of the north with 50,000 men, the god of the center with 100,000. In each of the sequences the entourage of disciples moves, sings the words, and burns the talismans. The high priest stands in the center meditating and seeing within his mind the process of renewal and rebirth, the "planting" of the revivifying breaths of the five directions. To the disciples, the high priest is summoning and controlling the universe and all its spirits; to the high priest himself, and the few trained in the esoteric meditations, the spirits symbolized in the *Ho-t'u*, the life-giving chart of the Prior Heavens, are restoring the cosmos to its pristine vigor of life, *Yang*, and blessing. The first step toward longevity, *Ch'ang-sheng*, and the continuing birth of *Yang* has been accomplished.

To understand the next step of the *Chiao* sequence of rituals, a number of obscure manuals must be noted. The cryptic *Yellow Court Canon* (*Huang-t'ing Ching*) is used by the Taoist master in training his disciples for the rituals which follow the *Su Ch'i*. The principles of the *Yellow Court Canon* will be abstracted in the brief passage which follows, as the Taoist master explains it.

## The Second Day

In the appendices of the *I-ching* describing the *Ho-t'u*, the chart of the Prior Heavens is said to depict the five elements in the order in which they give life. A further passage says, "East's 3 (wood) and south's 2 (fire) when brought together make 5 (ashes, or the earth of center). North's 1 (water) and west's 4 (metal) also come together (to make five). *Wu* and *Chi* (the earth of center), when returned to their origin (5), are based upon the number of life (birth); when one sees these three together [*i.e.*, by bringing the three fives together into the center] the red infant [immortal life] is formed."[34]

In the chart of the *Ho-t'u*, the five elements are united into three sets of five, or three fives; one recalls that the title of the Taoist "Three-Five Surveyors of Merit" referred to the five spirits of the Posterior Heavens, and to the Three Pure Ones, the Taoist Trinity. The Primordial Heavenly Worthy is lord of heaven, his color or vapor is blue-green, and he represents primordial breath. The second of the Three Pure Ones, the *Ling-pao* Heavenly Worthy, is lord of earth. He is a symbol for primordial spirit of center, and his color is yellow. Finally, the third of the Three Pure Ones, the *Tao-te* Heavenly Worthy or *Lao Tzu*, is lord of men; his color is white, and he represents seminal essence, the symbolization of metal and water. The Three Pure Ones can thus also be taken to represent the three fives; that is, Primordial Heavenly Worthy is the spirit of wood and fire combined (2+3);

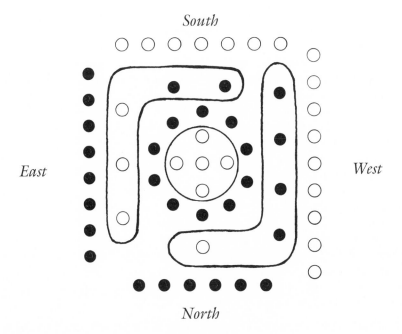

Figure 4. The *Ho-t'u* related to the school of interior meditation.

*Ling-pao* Heavenly Worthy is the spirit of earth (5); and *Tao-te* Heavenly Worthy is the spirit of water and metal combined (4+1). By bringing these three together into the center of the microcosm in interior meditation, and bringing them together into the center of the temple by ritual meditation, long life, continual birth, or longevity is obtained. The esoteric name for long life (continual birth) is the little red child, the *Ying-erh*.

A closer examination of the liturgy of renewal which is being performed by the Taoists during the *Chiao* ceremonies shows that they are doing precisely what was described in the passage above. On the second day of the celebration, during the Morning, Noon, and Night Audiences, the Taoist makes present the Three Pure Ones. On the last day he offers them a banquet in the center of the sacred *T'an* area, thus causing the "three fives" to be seen together at once in the center of the cosmos, the requisite condition for *Ch'ang-sheng*, continual life and blessing.

On the morning of the second day, between 3:00 and 5:00, the Taoist performs the Morning Audience.[35] During this ritual, the Taoist high priest sees the green breath of the east fill the macrocosm and the microcosm. He sees the bright green-blue light of the Primordial Heavenly Worthy's primordial breath fill the five organs of his body, the symbols in the microcosm of the five sacred peaks in the visible world. The five old emperors and all their retainers, the devout members of the village community, and the whole cosmos are filled with the primordial breath of wood and fire combined.

Late in the morning of the second day the Taoist performs the Noon Audience.[36] The rubrics say that this ceremony must be performed between 9:00 and 11:00 and be finished before noon in order to have effect. Thus the time of the day (noon), the yellow breath of center, and the *Ling-pao* Heavenly Worthy, lord of earth, are intimately related. The Taoist takes up his position in the center of the sacred area, and while the disciples perform the externals of the ritual, he again meditates on the gods of the Prior Heavens, as in the Morning Audience a few hours before. He sees the yellow breath of primordial spirit come forth from his spleen and fill the cosmos. The *Ling-pao* Heavenly Worthy is summoned to the center of the sacred *T'an* area by the *mudras* and *mantras* at the Taoist's command. The yellow breath of primordial spirit fills the macrocosm and the microcosm. Again the five organs with their five sets of spirits are imbued with the yellow, life-giving vapor. The yellow vapor of center is seen as the natural child or the object produced from the combination of wood and fire; thus wood and fire produce ashes, and so the primordial elements wood and fire produce the life-giving earth of center. The text of the Taoist canon warns that if the meditative ritual has not been completed by noon, the ceremony will have no effect.

Finally, in the afternoon of the second day of the *Chiao* festival of renewal, the Taoist performs the last of the three audiences, the Night Audience.[37] The rite is performed just at dusk, and the third of the Taoist Trinity, the *Tao-te* Heavenly Worthy, is summoned for an audience in the center of the sacred *T'an* area. The Taoist from his position in front of the altar in the center of the temple sees a white vapor arising from his lungs. The seminal essence of water and metal in combination is thus symbolized by the white mists filling the cosmos. The *Tao-te* Heavenly Worthy, by being present in the center of the sacred area, causes the life-giving powers of water and metal to fill the five organs, the five spirits, and all their retainers. The Taoist entourage, the devout members of the community present in the temple, and the whole village are renewed by the life-giving vapors.

The commentator on the text, a Sung dynasty Taoist *Chin Yün-chung*, says that these three vapors are the primordial breaths that formed the universe; they are the three palaces of the Three Pure Ones in the Prior

Heavens. The great Taoist scholars of the Tang dynasty (*Tu kuang-t'ing*) and of the Chin-liang dynasties (*Lu-Hsiu-ching*) both interpret the meditations of the three audiences to be based upon these three colors, green, yellow, and white. More recent Taoists (that is, in the Sung dynasty, namely the more heterodox *Shen-hsiao* orders, founded between 1119 and 1126) mistakenly meditate on the three colors red, yellow, and white. This error is due to mistaking the "wood-fire" elements of the meditation for the color of red (fire). The Sung dynasty commentator then explains that only illiterate or heterodox Taoists would make such a basic error. The gloss of the commentator *Chin Yün-chung* perhaps gives a deeper explanation of the terminology used by the common folk to identify the Taoists. The orthodox Heavenly Master sect *Cheng-i* Taoist is called a Black-head (*Wu-t'ou*) Taoist. He meditates on the color blue-green (*Hsüan* or purple-black is another term given to the vapor). Some of the Heavenly Master sect Red-head Taoists, the *Shen-hsiao* orders, on the other hand, meditate on the color red instead. The association of a color with the origin of the cosmos may thus be the basis which identifies two kinds of Taoists on Taiwan.

## The Third Day

Having brought the primordial breaths of the cosmos into the sacred area of the temple, as well as into the microcosm of the body, it remains for the Taoist to perform the final act of the festival of renewal. He must call together the Three Pure Ones for a banquet in the center, so that all three may be kept together, or "seen together" perpetually, thus concluding the alliance with the heavenly spirits and assuring the rebirth of the community. With the Three Pure Ones always in the center of the cosmos, *Yang* will always reign supreme and never be overcome by *Yin*. Primordial breath and seminal essence (represented by the first and third of the Heavenly Worthies) will not flow out and be dissipated. Spirit (the *Ling-pao* Heavenly Worthy) will always stay in the center of the cosmos (*i.e.*, the microcosm, the body), and the new life, called the *Ying-erh*, the hierophant, or the ruddy child, will be formed. The ceremony is accomplished on the last day of the *Chiao* festival. It is called either *Tao-ch'ang* (the mandala of the *Tao*) or the *Cheng Chiao*, the "True" or "Orthodox" *Chiao*. The form of the ritual is outwardly no different from that of other Taoist ceremonies. The mandala of the heavens are created by summoning the spirits from the Prior Heavens, and from the Taoist's body. All of the gods of the five directions, heaven, earth, and water (the three stages), the nine orifices, and the 366 joints of the body take up their positions around the sacred *T'an* area. The Taoists envision each of the spirits as present, seeing the colors and minutest details of the costume. Thereupon, the Three Pure Ones, present in their positions in the center of the area, are one by one offered incense and wine. It must be recalled here that the original meaning of *Chiao* is a sacrifice to the heavenly spirits, consisting of incense and wine only. Thus the purest spirits of the Prior Heavens are fed on the purest of foods, wine and incense. The rite is basically a banquet, following which the Taoists perform the stately steps of a heavenly ritual dance, to the accompaniment of ancient music. Finally, the petitions of the entire community are sent off by burning before the assembled deities.[38] At such an auspicious gathering, all the slightest wishes of the pious faithful are granted, the lost souls in the underworld are freed, and the blessing of *Yang* and life from the Prior Heavens is won for the coming generation.

The elite rituals of the *Chiao* festival of renewal are completed with the *Tao Ch'ang*, the banquet sacrifice making the Three Pure Ones present in the center of the microcosm. The rituals of the *Chiao* are by no means ended, as far as the people are concerned, however. The Taoist must still perform the solemn presentation of the petitions of the community to the Jade Emperor and the spirits of the Posterior Heavens in a ceremony in front of the temple. Following the presentation of the petitions, the great communal banquet called *P'u-tu* or "general crossing over" is held. A huge feast is laid out on tables in front of the temple. Uncooked meats are offered to the demons; cooked foods of all sorts are prepared for the freed ancestors and spirits; finally the men and women of the visible world sit down to a twenty-four-course meal, the first time that meat has been eaten during the week of abstinence preceding the last day of the festival. When heavenly gods, earthly and underworld spirits, and finally the village inhabitants and their guests have eaten their fill, the concluding ceremonies of the *Chiao* are held. The gods are thanked and sent off to the realms from which they came. The special temple decorations are dismantled, and the temple is restored to its original state. Just as the cosmos is renewed at the winter solstice to a state of life and blessing, so, too, the microcosm and the underworld of ancestors and spirits have been blessed for another cycle of a lifetime, or until the next *Chiao* celebration.

Perhaps the most remarkable aspect of the *Chiao* is its two-fold ritual structure. A set of rituals is performed behind the locked doors of the temple, for the gods of the Prior Heavens. These rituals are understood only by the Taoists, and in their fullness by the chief Taoist alone. It is the purpose of these elite rituals to win the blessing of the Prior Heavens, the return of the universe (macro- and microcosm) to the state of primordial *Yang* and continual birth. A second set of rituals, addressed to the spirits of the

Posterior Heavens, is seen and understood by the devout members of the community who patronize the temple and believe in the Chinese religion. These rites are seen as winning merit which forgives the evil actions of men stemming from *Yin*. Due to the rites, the souls are freed, blessing is won, and the prosperity of the village guaranteed for another generation. This second kind of ritual, which the Taoist performs for the benefit of the laymen and laywomen of the community during the *Chiao* festival, that is, which is performed in public and seen by the whole village, does not differ from the rites offered on the occasion of an annual festival or the birthday celebration in honor of a patron deity.

Furthermore, the rites offered by the Taoist and the Buddhist in temples patronized by the devout believers in Chinese religion do not differ basically in the structure or order of ritual. When the orders of ritual in the Buddhist monastery and the Chinese temple are compared, the resemblance is indeed startling. The following lists of rituals were performed on the Festival of the Water Spirits, on the fifteenth day of the tenth lunar month, in 1969, in Hsinchu county. The first set, performed at the Lionhead Mountain Buddhist monastery from 4:00 A.M. until noon, and the second set, done in the *Ch'eng Huang* temple in Hsinchu city from midafternoon until evening, were witnessed and recorded by the author:

| *Buddhist Monastery* | *Ch'eng Huang Temple* (Taoist priest) |
|---|---|
| Summoning the spirits | Summoning the spirits |
| Purifying the temple and participants | Purifying the temple |
| Lotus Sutra | Three Officials canon |
| Diamond Sutra | Pole Star canon |
| Three Officials canon | Southern Star canon |
| Pole Star canon | Three Origins canon |
| Three Origins canon | Food offering |
| Noon Offering | *Tao Ch'ang* (Three Offerings) |
| *P'u-tu* (Freeing the Souls) | *P'u-tu* (Freeing the Souls) |
| Thanking the *Buddha* | Thanking the spirits |

The program of rituals offered in the popular temples and in Buddhist monasteries of Taiwan generally follows the above outline. Purifications, acts of merit and repentance, the offering of food and mock paper money, the burning of incense, and finally the ritual act of freeing the souls are commonly found in rituals performed for the sake of devout adherents of the Chinese religion.

The rituals performed by the Taoist behind the locked doors of the temple, however, are quite different both in structure and in content from those performed in public, or shared with Buddhist rites offered for the sake of the faithful. The esoteric rites of the Taoist are based on the ritual of the

"Three Pure Ones," and the "*Ling-pao* Five Talismans," rituals which summon the gods of the Prior Heavens, the source of life, blessing, and happiness, to the center of the cosmos for an "Audience with the *Tao* of Transcendence." The ends and purposes of the popular religion are thus satisfied, that is, blessing is won and the souls of the ancestors are freed from the underworld. But the method used by the Taoist derives from the monastic interior meditation tradition, *i.e.*, "Interior Alchemy," as performed in ritual meditation in the mind of the Taoist, behind the locked doors of the village temple. In fact, the Taoist by his magical powers summons all of the spirits within the microcosm, which correspond to the three stages of the macrocosm, and purifies them for an encounter with the primordial spirits of the Prior Heavens. There is thus a relationship between the annual festival at the lunar New Year, the coming down of the heavenly spirits into the Chinese household, and the ritual which the Taoist performs during the *Chiao*. The gods of the visible world, in three stages, are removed from the central part of the temple. The gods of the Prior Heavens, the stellar constellations, are called down to take the place of the gods in the Posterior Heavens.

The Taoist, thereupon, applies the principles of interior alchemy, or ritual meditation, to establish a feudal contract with the life-bearing gods of the Prior Heavens through methods derived from the *Ts'an T'ung Ch'i*, the *Yellow Court Canon*, and the use of an ancient chart called *Ling-pao* Five Talismans, a kind of *Ho-t'u*. The five primordial spirits, who represent the five elements as giving life, are planted into the microcosm and the macrocosm. The Three Pure Ones, three aspects of the *Tao* of transcendence, are also made present in the microcosm. Finally a banquet for the three "In the Center of the Yellow Court," the source of life within man, is presented on the last day of the *Chiao* festival, sealing the treaty with the gods, renewing life for the coming generations, and freeing the souls from the underworld.

The purpose of the Taoist and the purpose of the faithful in offering the *Chiao* festival are not, in fact, dissimilar. The outcome of the *Chiao* festival of renewal, *Ch'ang-sheng* (longevity), was indeed won for all. In the sense that the souls suffering in the underworld are released and wafted to the heavens to become immortals, *Ch'ang-sheng* is indeed won for the departed. In the second sense of *Ch'ang-sheng*, where the two characters are taken to mean "continuing birth," the "planting" of the *Ho-t'u* or the marriage of the *Yin* and *Yang* aspects of the five elements in the microcosm wins blessing and continuing life for another generation. Finally, as a last act following the *Tao Ch'ang* and the presentation of the community's petitions, the Taoist posts a huge red document called *Pang* on the temple wall.  The *Pang* contains a list of names of every living member of the community who was involved in the *Chiao*, or who paid for the proceedings.  Their names are posted as if they were literati who had passed the imperial examinations and attained the rank of *Chin-shih*, doctors of letters.  They have in fact attained the ranks of immortal in the Prior Heavens.  Thus the end and purpose of the meditations of interior alchemy, *Ch'ang-sheng*, eternal life, have been achieved for the entire community.

# V

# Taoism in Modern China[1]

The *Chiao* ritual described in chapters two and four is typical of *Cheng-i Meng-wei* Taoism practiced in south Fukien province, Lung-hu Shan in Kiangsi, Mao Shan in Kiangsu, and other places on the China mainland. It should be understood, however, that there are many other kinds of *Chiao* rituals and Taoist practices not treated in the above pages. Chapter five examines the origins and kinds of *Chiao* ritual, and their manifestations in modern Chinese practice. Taoism can be compared to a great river whose waters, fed by many streams and lesser rivers, tumble into the vast ocean. Some of these waters are tasted in chapter five.

The history of Taoism in China has been divided by modern scholars into seven eras:[2]

1.   The period of gestation from *Lao-tzu* in the sixth century B.C., to the Huan-ti reign years, 147-168 A.D., and the introduction of the Taoist *T'ai-p'ing Ching-ling Shu* at court by *Hsaing Kai* and the Imperial sacrifice to *Lao-tzu* at Ku-hsien (165 A.D.). During this period, the works of *Lao-tzu* and *Chuang-tzu* were compiled. The *Huai-nan-tzu* integrated Taoist thought with *Yin-Yang* five-element cosmology and astronomy, and Taoist recluses such as the three *Mao* brothers of Mao Shan performed meditation and healing.

2.   The period of birth, 168-400 A.D., from the founding of the *T'ai-p'ing* movement in eastern China and Celestial Master Taoism in western China, until the passing of the first masters of Mao Shan. During this period, *Chang Tao-ling*, his son, and grandson founded what later became *Cheng-i Meng-wei* theocratic Taoism; the *Ko* family, *Hsü Ling-ch'i*, and others developed *Ling-pao* liturgical Taoism; *Yang Hsi*, the two *Hsü's*, father and son, and others established Mao Shan *Shang-ch'ing* meditative Taoism.

3.   The period of growth, 400-580 A.D., from the end of the *Sun En* rebellion, 402 A.D., to the beginning of the Sui dynasty. *Ling-pao*, *Shang-ch'ing*, and *Meng-wei* Taoism grew during this period and became part of a common Taoist legacy. *Lu Hsiu-ching* catalogued the first Taoist canon.

4.   The period of maturation, 581-907 A.D.: the Sui/T'ang period. During this time Taoism was officially recognized and patronized by the T'ang court, and *Lao-tzu* was included in Imperial examinations. Princesses received Taoist investiture. *Shang-ch'ing* meditation,

*Ling-pao* liturgy, and *Cheng-i* registers were ranked first, second, and third in Taoist investiture practice.

5. The period of reformation and division, 907-1368 A.D. Reform Taoism, led by the *Ch'uan-chen* (All Truth) sect, integrated *Ch'an* (Zen) Buddhist meditation and Neo-Confucian thought with religious Taoism. New forms of Taoist practice now ranked *Shang-ch'ing* meditation highest, followed by *Ch'ing-wei* Thunder (tantric), Pole Star, *Cheng-i Meng-wei*, and *Ling-pao*.

6. The period of decline, 1368-1979 A.D. The Ming and Ch'ing dynasties controlled and opposed Taoism. The Japanese burn Mao Shan and kill the Taoists (1938). Taoism is preserved on Taiwan.

7. The period of rebirth, 1979 to the present. Ritual Taoism is suppressed in the People's Republic of China (PRC), 1949-1979, but grows and flourishes in modern Taiwan. The freedom of religion clause promulgated in 1979 sees an astonishing rebirth of religion in the PRC, with the reappearance of monastic and popular ritual Taoism in the 1980s.[3]

Investigations conducted in recent decades on Taiwan by modern scholars brought about a new interest in the study of Chinese religion. On Taiwan, the folk religion and ritual Taoism originally brought by the Ming and Ch'ing dynasty settlers from across the Taiwan straits hundreds of years ago has continued to flourish.[4] Consequently, scholars from America, Europe, and Japan flocked to Taiwan to analyze the popular *Chiao* rituals performed during village festivals.[5] The difference between the *Ling-pao* rituals of south Taiwan and the *Cheng-i Meng-wei* liturgies of north Taiwan represent important distinctions also found across the straits in Fukien province on the China mainland. However, the great mainland centers preserved other liturgical traditions, such as monastic celibacy and the ascetic life, not found in the practices of Taiwan's "fire-dwelling" or married Taoists. These traditions can now be studied in the People's Republic of China, and are discussed below.

Recent surveys in the PRC, however, show that Taoist liturgy is much more complex than heretofore thought by Western, Japanese, or Chinese scholars whose research was confined to Taiwan. An attempt will be made here to explain some of these differences and relate the Taoism of Taiwan to its origins on the mainland. The research for this update was conducted between May 1987 and August 1988, and covers those areas in Fukien province from which the Taiwanese Taoists originated. The great monastic centers Lung-hu Shan, Mao Shan, and Wu-tang Shan, mentioned so frequently in Taiwan Taoist texts, were included in the survey. The Taoists of Tainan, for instance, are closest to the traditions of southern Fukien province, while the *Cheng-i Szu-t'an* of north Taiwan recite documents found at Lung-hu Shan, Mao Shan, and Wu-tang Shan in more northern China.

The first studies of Taoism of Taiwan, published by the Japanese during the colonial period (1895-1945) and confirmed in various local gazeteers

(Taiwan *T'ung-chih*) between 1870 and 1970, show that Taoists were classified as either Red-head (Mandarin dialect: *Hung-t'ou*; Min or Taiwan dialect: *Ang-thau*) or Black-head (Mandarin: *Wu-t'ou*; Min: *O-thau*). The popular definition of Red and Black Taoists is simple and universal, *i.e.*, Red-head Taoists perform rituals for the living, while Black-head Taoists do the same but also conduct burial services for the dead. Recent surveys in Chang-chou of Fukien province, just across the straits, have shown that an analogous classification is used in this traditional city where Taoists are classified as "Ang" (Red) and "O" (Black).[6]

Further analysis of field evidence, derived in north as well as south Taiwan, has shown that several kinds of Red and Black Taoists exist in the north, while a simpler distinction holds true for the Taoists of Tainan and in the south. In north Taiwan, Red-head refers to all Taoists who perform rituals for the living, and all rituals performed by these Taoists are classified as Red-head rituals. These groups and their rituals include the following:

   1.    Red-head *Ling-pao* Taoists: liturgical descendants of the *Liu* clan from Changchou, Fukien province, who perform a classical form of *Chiao* ritual as described in these pages.
   2.    Red-head *Lü-shan* Taoists, who wrap a red cloth around their heads when performing exorcisms and healing, and blow on a cow-horn trumpet. These Taoists are liturgically descendants of the *Lin* clan from southern Fukien province and work with the *Sannai* (Three Sisters) possessed mediums (Min dialect: *Tang-ki*). The *Lü-shan* Taoists act as interpreters of trance mediums, do healing-exorcist ceremonies, and perform a *Chiao* ritual quite unlike the *Ling-pao* rites of the *Liu* style liturgists or the Black-head *Meng-wei* Taoists.[7]
   3.    Though the *Lü-shan* Taoists do not call themselves *Shen-hsiao*, the style of *Chiao* liturgy they perform is classified as *Shen-hsiao* by some of the elder teachers of the tradition and by the Black-head Taoists who watch them perform.[8] The *Shen-hsiao* liturgies of renewal (or Red-head *Chiao* of north Taiwan of the *Lin* clan tradition) do not use the classical *An Chen-wen* rite for planting the five talismans, nor the *Shou Chen-wen* rite for harvesting the talismans and internalizing (planting) them in the interior organs of the body, as described in chapter four.[9]

Likewise, the Black-head Taoists of Taiwan classify themselves into more than one order or style of liturgy, according to the registers or *Lu* that they have received from a master. The registers that Taoists learn are many, the most important of which are the following:

   1.    The *Ling-pao San-wu Tu-kung* register (Tainan, south Taiwan).
   2.    The *Cheng-i Meng-wei* register (Hsinchu, north Taiwan).
   3.    The *Pei-chi Hsüan-wu* register (north and south Taiwan).
   4.    The *Ch'ing-wei* (*Wu-lei Fa*) register (Hsinchu, north Taiwan).
   5.    The *Shang-ch'ing* (Mao Shan) register: *Yellow Court Canon*.

We may wonder what these registers consist of, and, indeed, the very fact that a Taoist claims to know a register does not mean that he or she is expert in its use. In general, the register gives the Taoist the right to perform a certain kind of ritual. For example, the *Ling-pao San-wu Tu-kung* register is the basic knowledge required of a Taoist master to perform as the high priest at a *Chiao*. This role is called *Kao-kung Fa-shih*, *i.e.*, the Master of Exalted Merit, and presumes that the Taoist can perform the *Fa-lu* rite for summoning spirits and building the sacred spiritual area in which the *Chiao* liturgies are performed as described in chapter four. All Taoists who perform the *Chiao* liturgies of renewal know the *Fa-lu* rite, since it occurs in the texts used during village ritual. The manner of performing the *Fa-lu* varies according to the order and rank of the Taoist.[10]

An investigation of the great mainland centers of Taoist learning prove that Taoists are ranked according to the registers they have learned. In fact, from the Sung dynasty onward, if not earlier (Sui and T'ang dynasty evidence shows that Taoists were classified according to the registers they had acquired),[11] the central government of China required that Taoists be licensed according to the registers they actually knew how to use in liturgy. The three great Taoist centers, Mao Shan in Kiangsu and Lung-hu Shan and Ko-tsao in Kiangsi, were granted by imperial favor the right to examine the registers of local Taoists, teach new registers, and sell licenses permitting Taoists to perform liturgy in the public forum. Taoists so licensed were called *San Shan Ti-hsüeh P'ai* (The Order of the Three Mountain Blood Alliance), a title that appears on the ordination manual used at Lung-hu Shan up to today.[12]

The ordination manual used by the Three Mountain Alliance, entitled *Chi-lu T'an-ching Yüan K'o* (Original Ordination Manual for Giving the Register, Altar, and Meditation Room Title), ranks Taoists into nine grades, analogous to the nine official ranks of the Confucian Mandarinate. The titles, in association with a forty-character poem identifying rank for members of the Three Mountain Alliance, are as follows:[13]

1.    Grade One Taoist: knowledge of the *San-ch'ing Ta-t'ung Lu*, *i.e.*, the *Huang-t'ing Ching Yellow Court Canon*, and the other texts of the Mao Shan *Shang-ch'ing* tradition.
2.    Grade Two and Three Taoist: knowledge of the *San-tung Wu-lei Ching-lu*, *i.e.*, the Three Arcana Five Thunder Registers and Canons.[14]
3.    Grade Four and Five Taoist: knowledge of the twenty-four *Cheng-i Meng-wei Ching-lu* registers.[15]
4.    Grade Six and Seven Taoist: knowledge of the *T'ai-shang San-wu Tu-kung Ching-lu*, *i.e.*, the *T'ai-shang Ling-pao* Three-five Surveyor of Merit Register and Canons, including the manuals, oral instructions, and paraphernalia for performing the *Chiao* liturgy of renewal and the rites of burial.
5.    Grade Eight and Nine Taoist are not listed in the manual. These grades, according to the oral traditions of the Three Mountain Alliance, are given to acolytes, scholars, and novices who study liturgy, music, sacred dance, and monastic asceticism, but are not yet qualified or licensed to perform the role of *Kao-kung Fa-shih* (Master of Exalted Merit) in the *Chiao* liturgy.

The Taoists of the *Cheng-i Szu-t'an* tradition of north Taiwan have preserved and transmitted the liturgies and meditations of Grades Two through Six ordination (the *Cheng-i Meng-wei*, *San-tung Wu-lei* and *San-wu Tu-kung* registers) listed above. The Hsinchu branch of the alliance also transmits the *Yellow Court Canon* and its meditations and uses a special Yellow Court liturgy during the *Chiao* rite of renewal. Meditations in the Mao Shan *Shang-ch'ing*, Pole Star Sword, and *Ch'ing-wei* Five Thunder register traditions are taught along with the music, ritual dance, and liturgies of this relatively young alliance of Taoists in north Taiwan. The present master, *Chuang Chia-hsin*, is in his early forties and most of the thirty or so aspirants, novices, and cantors are in their late twenties. The tradition will flourish into the next century, since interest among the younger generation of Taiwanese intellectuals and businessmen is growing, rather than decreasing, with modernization in Taiwan.

The Red-head and Black-head Taoists of Tainan city in south Taiwan seem to transmit simpler forms of the registers than their northern brothers. The scholars who have studied the *Chiao* ritual of the renowned *Ch'en* family of Tainan do not go beyond a purely "etic" or external view of the rites, and make no mention of internal meditation or other data deriving from registers higher than the *San-wu Tu-kung* (Grade Six) *Ching-lu*.[16] Pending further investigation of the Taoist masters of Kaohsiung and other southern cities, the Grade Six *San-wu Tu-kung* rank Black-head Taoists and the simple *Lü-shan* Red-head Taoists who wrap a red cloth around the head and exorcise with a cow-horn trumpet seem more common in south Taiwan. The Taoist ritual practices of Taiwan are, however, at the present time, among the most authentic found in modern China.

With the promulgation of the freedom of religion clause in 1979, the People's Republic of China has witnessed a revival of religious practices. The five great traditions, Buddhist, Catholic and Protestant Christian, Islam, and Taoism, experienced significant growth after a period of suppression and destruction.[17] Religion, the central government has now declared, is not incompatible with the goals of the socialist state, since both support morality, ethics, loyalty to the nation, and increased productivity. The repairing of religious shrines destroyed during the Cultural Revolution (1966-1976), the opening of seminaries for training priests, monks, nuns, ministers, and mullahs at state expense, and the restoration of public religious services has placed China at the front of the modern socialist states in this regard.

Taoism is experiencing a growth and revitalization at a crucial time. The Red Guard, during the Cultural Revolution, destroyed many time-honored temples, monasteries, and mountaintop retreats. With the exception of the shrines of Wu-tang Shan in Hupei province and the remnants of T'ang history found on Ch'ing-ch'eng Shan near Cheng-tu city in Szechuan province, almost all of the great Taoist centers were ravaged and the Taoists dispersed. The renewed popularity of these places as sites for pilgrimages and festivals, however, now assures their restoration.

Mao Shan near Nanjing has suffered more than any other center. In 1938, forty or more temples were destroyed, over a thousand Taoists were killed or scattered, and the original woodblocks of the Sung dynasty canon were burned by the Japanese. Attempts to restore the buildings and recover parts of the canon in the 1950s were obliterated by the events of 1966-1976. The ruins of the Wan-fu Kung temple atop the highest peak and a few rooms in the Yin-kung monastery near the caves once made famous by medieval alchemists and recluses were the only relics left from the glorious past.

Yet today Mao Shan has five elderly masters, sixty novices, and over 10,000 pilgrims a day attending the larger festivals. The author was permitted to ascend to the peak of the great Mao Shan a total of six times between May 1987 and August 1988 and witness the deep lasting role that Taoism plays in the hearts of the peasants. Copies of the *Chiao* liturgies celebrated by the Mao Shan masters and their disciples are now available on cassette tapes and sold at mainland and Hong Kong bookstores. Visitors to the mountain in springtime (from Chinese New Year through the fifteenth day of the third lunar month) and on other special occasions, may still see the *Shang-ch'ing Chiao* and hear the classical melodies preserved by the Mao Shan masters. The similarity of the music of Mao Shan with that of the *Cheng-i Szu-t'an* of Hsinchu, Taiwan, is striking.

The elderly Master *Shih Ta-te* of Mao Shan uses the twenty-ninth poetic character *Ta* in his Taoist title and teaches the *Shang-ch'ing, Ling-pao, Pei-chi*, and *Wu-lei* registers with a Grade Three rank. The *Pei-chi* and *Wu-lei* (Pole Star and Five Thunder) registers are identical with those used by the *Cheng-i Szu-t'an* Taoists of north Taiwan.[18] Both *Shih* and the younger master *Chou* claim to know the *Yellow Court Canon* meditations, but his manual, along with many of the *K'o-i* rites used during the *Chiao*, were burned by the Red Guard. The Mao Shan rituals are being rewritten from memory by the older Taoists, but funds are needed to buy the Shanghai reprint of the *Cheng-t'ung* Taoist canon.

Master *Shih* performs the *An Chen-wen* meditation of the *Ling-pao* Five True Writs (as described in chapter four) during the Morning Audience, instead of during the *Su-ch'i* ritual, a practice which differs from that of the Taoists of Taiwan and south Fukien. In regard to the local variants in ritual style found throughout China, *Shih* claimed that the inner structure of *Chiao* liturgy (*Chiao-shih De Gou-tsao*) was important, but the sequence of ritual could be changed (*K'o-yi Tiao-huan*) according to local custom. The Mao Shan masters also carry a special manual called *Huang-shu* (Yellow Book) in which many forms of ritual practice and meditation are recorded for oral transmission to the Mao Shan disciples. *Shih* does not teach the oral secrets to the young Taoists until they have *Ting-hsin*, i.e., quieted their hearts and minds by living in the Yin-kung monastery and practicing prayer, song, and breathing meditation. The Taoists who make a living off the tourists in Wan-fu Kung atop Mao Shan are excluded from this transmission.

Wu-tang Shan, in western Hupei province near the Shensi border, is a grueling four-day journey from Shanghai and Nanjing.[19] Over 1,000 people a day visit this scenic spot while on Taoist pilgrimages. Protected by direct orders of *Chou En-lai* from the rampaging Red Guard, the grounds of the 4,600-feet-high monastery yet maintain its Ming dynasty splendor. The buildings, statues, and monuments funded by the Yung-lo emperor (1403-1424 A.D.) are nestled aesthetically in one of the most scenic locations in China. Towering peaks, caves for recluses, vegetable gardens, and stele (stone monuments) recording *Chiao* ceremonies for past emperors create an authentic image of traditional Taoist life at its best.

Some thirty Taoists, fifty young monks, and twenty young nuns live a celibate, vegetarian, contemplative life according to the *Ch'uan-chen* monastic rules. The *Chiao* rites of the Three Mountain Drop of Blood Alliance are preserved by Taoist Master *La-pa* (Trumpet), who in his eighty-fourth year teaches the drumming, singing, music, and dancing of a combined *Ch'uan-chen* and *Cheng-i Chiao* liturgy. Master *La-pa's Chiao* has been video-recorded, and the Taoist music is available on cassette tape at mainland and Hong Kong bookstores. *Cheng-i* and *Pei-chi* (Pole Star) Taoists no longer live within the monastic complex, which is exclusively occupied by the reformed *Ch'uan-chen* order. But the foothills around the mountain, from Wu-tang Shan, through Shih-yen, Hsiang-fan, to Wuhan city, support fire-dwelling married Taoists who use the *Cheng-i* form of *Chiao* liturgy. Since state law requires that Taoist rituals performed for the public must take place within a temple, the *Cheng-i* Taoists use traditional Ch'uan-chen monasteries, such as the Ch'ang-ch'uan Kuan (Eternal Spring) temple in Wuhan city, to perform *Chiao* festivals and burials.

The traditions of the Celestial Master and the *Cheng-i Meng-wei* tradition are preserved at T'ien-shih Fu, San-ch'ing village, Lung-hu Shan, in Kiangsi province. A seventeen-hour ride by train from Nanjing, or thirteen hours from Hsiamen, the headquarters of *Cheng-i* Taoism is located in the quiet beauty of the original temple complex, supported by the memorabilia of Sung dynasty emperors.[20] Eight elderly Taoists preserve the *Chiao* festival of the *Cheng-i* tradition, and pass on the registers and liturgical teachings from father to son and master to disciple as in the past. The *Chiao* rites and music have been recorded by the Kiangsi provincial government, but are not yet available at the time of this writing. The Taoists, however, are quite willing to have the *Chiao* ritual photographed and recorded by scholars. The elderly Taoist *Wang Shao-lin* resides in the temple complex as the ritual expert Celestial Master, following the time-honored *Cheng-i* saying:

*Wang pu li Chang, Chang pu li Wang*
(Wang stays with Chang; Chang stays with Wang!)

The *Wang* family Taoists have been ritual instructors for the Celestial Master since the late Sung dynasty according to Lung-hu Shan records.[21] Manuals purchased at Lung-hu Shan between 1868 and 1888 by Taoists from Hsinchu in north Taiwan bear the signature of the *Wang* masters who taught Taoist ritual there during the Ch'ing dynasty. Comparing Taiwan manuals with the Lung-hu Shan texts used by *Wang Shao-lin*, it was possible to verify that Red-head and Black-head Taoists did come to the Celestial Master to purchase manuals, registers, and documents to perform ritual. The Three Mountain Drop of Blood Alliance and its manual are still used to train Taoists who come to Lung-hu Shan.

When asked about the five kinds of Taoists recognized in the Taiwan manuals, *Wang Shao-lin* acknowledged registers and grades found in the *Chi-lu T'an-ch'ing Yüan-k'o* and gave a heated explanation about the *Shen-hsiao* and other popular orders that came to Lung-hu Shan for registration and an official license. (The heavy rural accent of *Wang* was not easy to understand, so I insisted that he write out his remarks in my field notebook.) "The Shen-hsiao order," he wrote, "is a heterodox teaching [Hsieh Chiao]. The purpose of Lung-hu Shan is to correct the errors of the popular Taoists with the correct registers and rituals of Cheng-i Taoism." Taoists who come to Lung-hu Shan are allowed to write out the "correct" manuals for a fee and take them back to their villages.

The classification of Taoists found in the *Tao-chiao Yüan Liu* manual of Taiwan lists five major orders as follows:[22]

1.   The *Yü-ching* order (Mao Shan *Shang-ch'ing* Taoists).
2.   The *T'ien-shu* order (other monastic Taoists).[23]
3.   The *Pei-chi* Pole Star registers, of Wu-tang Shan.
4.   The *Yü-fu* registers, *i.e.*, the *Cheng-i* style liturgy promulgated at Lung-hu Shan and licensed to local Taoists.[24]
5.   The *Shen-hsiao* Taoists and their style of liturgy.[25]

Despite discrimination by *Wang Shao-lin* and other Black-head Taoists against *Shen-hsiao* liturgy, this popular style of blessing, healing, and exorcism continues to flourish in Taiwan with or without the title *Shen-hsiao*. *Wang Shao-lin* has manuals at Lung-hu Shan that were used to license the *Shen-hsiao* and other popular Taoists. I microfilmed this series, and shortly afterwards compared prints of these documents with the Taoist materials of north Taiwan. Red-head (*Huang, Ch'ien,* and *Ch'iu*) and Black-head (*Chuang* and others of the *Cheng-i Szu t'an*) Taoists of Hsinchu recognized the texts and specifically referred to them as *Shen-hsiao* style. The young leader of the Red-head *Ch'ien* clan confirmed that it was necessary to go again to Lung-hu Shan to compare the Taiwan texts with the originals, in case errors in copying had occurred since the journeys of Hsinchu Taoists in the late Ch'ing period. (I assured the young *Ch'ien*, however, that the Lung-hu Shan Taoists would be more concerned to copy the original materials of the Taiwan Taoists, since so much had been lost at Lung-hu Shan during the destructive Red Guard era. Taiwan now stands in the unique position as preserver and teacher in the long history of Taoism in China.)

Having recognized the five styles of liturgy listed above and the preservation of these styles in the magnificent *Chiao* ritual and the manuals preserved in north and south Taiwan, it now is possible to return to southern Fukien province and investigate the origins of Red-head and Black-head Taoism. A thirteen-hour train ride from Lung-hu Shan into southeast Fukien brings the traveler to the city of Changchou from whence many of the migrants to Taiwan came. The distinction of Black for burial ritual and Red for life ceremonies is clearly observed in Changchou. The Red-head Taoist *Liu* clan is well-known in the Changchou area, from the city of Lung-hai towards Hsiamen. Their ancestors were licensed at Lung-hu Shan in Kiangsi.[26] The manuals used by Master *Liu* for the *Chiao* ritual are identical to those of the *Cheng-i Szu-t'an* in Hsinchu. The Su-ch'i, Morning, Noon, and Night Audiences and the *Tao-ch'ang* rite as recorded in chapter four are common to the Changchou, Taiwan, and the Three Mountain Drop of Blood Alliance. The *Liu* clan head recalls visits of the Celestial Master to Changchou to visit his family.

A six-hour bus ride through the fertile coastal areas of southern Fukien brings the traveler to the modern city of Chuanchou from whence residents of north Taiwan emigrated. Famous for the T'ang dynasty *K'ai-yüan* Buddhist temple and the Sung dynasty Islamic mosque, Chuanchou has a thriving temple to the patron of merchants, *Kuan-kung*, and shrines to the Spirit of the Soil, *T'u-ti Kung*, in many street side shops and restaurants. The

Black-head Taoist *Ch'en* clan, who reside next to the Tung-yüeh Kung, the Temple of the Eastern Peak, perform rites and a *Chiao* ritual analogous to the *Cheng-i Szu t'an* of north Taiwan.[27]

Another four-hour ride by bus inland, through fields and hills dotted with shrines to the Spirit of the Soil, brings the traveler to the city and district of Anhsi, famous for the shrine to a holy T'ang dynasty monk, *Ch'ing-shui Tsu-shih* (Master Pure Water). Here the Black-head *Li* clan maintains the traditions of the *Huang-lu Chai* burial ritual and the *Cheng-i Meng-wei* register. In the future, a more thorough survey of south Fukien and north Kwangtung where the Min dialect is spoken will continue to show the relevance of the Three Mountain Drop of Blood Alliance, which exerts influence from Mao Shan and Wu-tang Shan in the north to Lung-hu Shan and the provinces of southeast China and Taiwan. The Taoists of this vast area are united by common registers, rituals, and the forty-character poem that identifies the generation by generation transmission of Taoist lore.[28]

We must now ask whether or not the Three Mountain Alliance is united together in more ways than by registers, titles, and identifying characters from a forty character poem. The *Chiao* rituals celebrated throughout southeast, central, and west China do, in fact, share many common aspects. As already noted, village, county, and provincial level Taoist associations in China have video-recorded the *Chiao* festivals of mainland China. These recordings and field survey notes can now be compared with recordings made of north and south Taiwan Taoist rituals. Studies by the Shanghai Academy of Social Sciences, for instance, have shown specific similarities between the *Chin-piao* rite for sending a memorial to the heavens and the *P'u-tu* liturgy for freeing all souls from a Buddhist inspired hell.[29] Since a *Chiao* ritual may have as many as 300 greater or lesser ceremonies squeezed into a brief three- or five-day period, we may ask whether or not some sort of liturgical order can be found within the system itself to determine the sequence and choice of liturgies to be used in the *Chiao* festival.

In my "Introduction" to *Chuang-lin Hsü Tao-tsang* (1975), I listed the different rituals found in the Black-head and Red-head *Chiao* festivals of north Taiwan.[30] Later studies of Hong Kong *Ch'uan-chen* Taoism and mainland monasteries provided additional information for an accurate portrayal of the Three Mountain Alliance and its local variants of the *Chiao*.[31]

The liturgies used in the *Chiao* festivals of the Three Mountain Alliance and the reformed *Ch'uan-chen* Taoists can be divided into three distinct styles, which are distinguished by their internal structure as follows:

1. The "A" theme rituals of a popular nature, shared by the Three Mountain, *Ch'uan-chen*, and the local Red-head or popular Taoist sects.

2. The "B" theme *Ch'ing* and *Ch'an* canons of merit and repentance that resemble Buddhist *sutra* chanting, but contain Taoist ideas. "B" liturgies are shared by all Taoists.

3. The "C" theme of classical or canonical liturgies that are based on the meditations of internal alchemy. This third genre of *Chiao* rituals is taught by the Three Mountain Alliance Taoists. Local Taoist masters go to Mao Shan, Ko-tsao Shan, and Lung-hu Shan to learn and be licensed in "C" style liturgy. As a general rule, all *Ling-pao*, *Cheng-i*, and *Shang-ch'ing* Taoists know and follow the meditations of inner alchemy.

Examples of the three styles are listed here, with rules for identifying the "A," "B," and "C" type rituals according to internal structure. The rules for teaching rituals in the "A" or "C" category are strictly followed at Lung-hu Shan and Mao Shan, since knowledge of the canonical meditations of internal alchemy and use of these meditations in liturgy are required for gaining Grade Six and higher ordination titles. "A" theme rites include all liturgies aimed at the balancing of human activity with the cycling motion of *Yin* and *Yang* in nature. Liturgies that are dramatic, filled with song and dance, exorcistic, healing, and send-off memorials, or act out passages of Taoist texts all belong to the "A" style of liturgy.

"B" theme liturgies are entitled *Ch'ing* for a canon to be chanted for merit or *Ch'an* for a litany of repentance.[32] Buddhists also use these terms, though the content of the Buddhist canons of merit and repentance are, of course, different. The goal of all "B" theme liturgies is the attaining of merit, and the freeing of the souls of the departed from the punishment of a bureaucratically complex hell that resembles a corrupt civil administration. The concluding rite, found in all *Chiao* liturgies, whether Red-head, Black-head, or reformed (*Ch'uan-chen*), is the *P'u-tu* liturgy for freeing all souls from hell.[33]

The "C" style liturgy uses internal alchemy, *i.e.*, breath and color meditation leading to a union with the *Tao. Hsin-chai* or abstaining from heart-mind activity, and *Tso-wang*, sitting in forgetfulness, are forms of meditation used by Taoists as methods for union with the *Tao, Yü Tao Ho-i.* Kenosis, or emptying of the heart and mind of all images, desires, and judgments, is a necessary requisite leading to union with the *Tao.* The above terms (all found in the *Chuang-tzu Nei-p'ien*, the inner chapters one through seven) are the basis of "C" style liturgy, during which the rites of the *Chiao* festival act out the process of kenotic, or emptying meditation. *Wei Tao chi hsü* (Only the *Tao* dwells in the void) are the words of the meditating Taoist master, echoing the fourth chapter of *Chuang-tzu.*[34] When performing the rite that acts out the process of union, the Taoists who follow the "C" style ritual sequence often suspend a scroll from the *T'an* altar with the words *Yü Tao Ho-i* (Let us join as one with the *Tao*!) drawn in gold calligraphy.

We can therefore identify three styles of *Chiao* ritual on the China mainland that are similar to, if not identical with, the *Chiao* liturgies of Taiwan. These are: (1) the popular *Chiao* rituals of the village Taoists that do not use the meditations of internal alchemy;[35] (2) the stately *Chiao* liturgies of the *Ch'uan-chen* monastic Taoists practiced at Wu-tang Shan, Pai-yün Kuan in Beijing, and in Hong Kong (the winning of heaven's blessing and the freeing of souls from hell are major goals of the *Ch'uan-chen Chiao* liturgy); and (3) the Three Mountain Alliance *Chiao* liturgies that do use the meditations of internal alchemy as part of the classical rites of union with the *Tao*, as described in these pages. The differences in these three styles may seem quite insignificant to the "etic" or external viewer untrained in the oral tradition of Taoist interior meditation.

Thus, the *Chiao* may be variously interpreted to be an "opening of a way" into the underworld, a general freeing of souls, the sending off of a memorial bearing the people's petitions to the heavens, or the manipulating of nature's governing spirits to win blessing.[36] Such a description adequately depicts the "A" and "B" themes presented above. But it does not do justice to the depth of meaning found in the "C" theme liturgies, as celebrated in the Three Mountain Alliance tradition. This tradition usually is taught only to disciples who have been accepted by a master and have learned how to do Taoist meditation (*"Ting-hsin"* as Master *Shih* of Mao Shan put it). Consequently, a scholar conducting scientific investigations in this area may find it necessary to be accepted as a student of a Taoist master and actually practice ritual meditation in order to experience the "emic" approach to esoteric ritual. Such an approach would classify most regular *Chiao* rituals as follows:

I. The "A" style liturgies, shared by all Taoists.
    1. *Fa Piao*, announcing the *Chiao* ritual to the cosmos.
    2. *Ch'ing Shen*, inviting the spirits to be present.
    3. *Chin T'an*, purifying the sacred *T'an* area for the *Chiao*.
    4. *Wu Hung*, Noontime Offering (performed each day).
    5. The *Fen Teng* rite (light lamps); act out *Lao-tzu*, chapter 42.
    6. Rite to the Pole Star (Pole Star register dance).
    7. Rites to the hearth spirit, dragon spirit, soil spirit.
    8. Rite to expel spirits of pestilence.
    9. Rite to thank and see off the spirits.

II. The "B" style liturgies to free all souls from hell. This style of liturgy also is shared by all Taoists.
    1. Canonical chant of merit to the Pole Star(s).
    2. Canonical chant of merit to the Three Sources (*San-yüan*).
    3. Canonical chant of merit to the Three Officials (*San-kuan*).
    4. Litanies of repentance to the heavens (ten volumes).

5. Litanies of repentance to the water spirits.
6. Rite for scattering flowers (merit to free souls).
7. *P'u-shih* (Buddhist *Yü-lan P'en*) to free all souls.

III. The classical "C" style of the Three Mountain Alliance Taoists.
1. The rite for planting the *Ling-pao* Five True Writs (sometimes celebrated during the *Su-ch'i* Night Announcement rite).
2. The morning rite for refining breath.
3. The noon rite for refining *Shen*-spirit.
4. The night rite for refining seminal (intuitive) essence.
5. The *Tao-ch'ang* or *Cheng-chiao* rite for union with the *Tao.*

Since the publishing of the first edition of *Taoism and the Rite of Cosmic Renewal* (1972), it is surprising that so many books and articles have been written about ritual Taoism that were based on some form of field studies and yet remained unaware of some basic Taoist meditative practices. The rules for transmitting oral Taoist teachings are strictly adhered to by most masters. Yet field work studies, based on a solid foundation in French structuralist method, should have noted that the planting (*an*, literally, planting or establishing the famous *Ling pao* Five True Writs) occurred always with the Morning, Noon, and Night Audiences, and ended with the *Tao ch'ang* rite for union with the *Tao* and the *shou* (harvesting) of the five *Ling-pao* True Writs.

As stated earlier, the Taoists suspend a scroll from the altar stating that *Yü Tao Ho-i* (Let us join as one with the *Tao!*) is the goal of the "C" theme liturgies. Whether called *Su-ch'i* and *Tao-ch'ang* as described in chapter four or by some other name, the structure of the rituals, *i.e.*, the order in which they are performed, the alchemical refinement of the Five (True Writs) to the Three (breath, spirit, essence), and the Three to the One to effect union with the *Tao*, is a common factor in all "C" style liturgies. This order of meditation and internal alchemy is observed in all of the mainland and Taiwan Taoist communities that belong to the Three Mountain Alliance. (The interested student need not travel to China to watch the *Chiao*, since videotapes of the "C" theme liturgies can now be purchased and viewed in the classroom or at home.)[37]

Of course, the variety and types of Taoist practices in mainland China include far more than just the complicated liturgical and ritual expressionism found in the *Chiao* ceremony. Taoists of the *Ch'uan-chen* sect are found throughout China practicing internal alchemy, Zen-like meditative sitting and breath circulation, and *T'ai-chi Kung-fu* exercise. The classical meditations of emptying, found in the Mao Shan *Yellow Court Canon* tradition, are also practiced, though less widely known. This cryptic work, which teaches the meditations of internal alchemy in the earlier *Wai-Chuan* and the exteriorizing or "emptying" of the bodily spirits and mental images in the later *Nei Chuan*, follows the same structural rules for union with the *Tao* as do the "C" theme liturgies of the Three Mountain Alliance. Taoists of this alliance chant the *Yellow Court Canon* on the last night of the *Chiao*, on the evening before the *Tao-ch'ang* meditation of union is performed.[38]

Finally, there are Taoists in China who simply meditate in the time-honored tradition of the *Lao-tzu* and *Chuang-tzu* recluses. I am deeply indebted to Professor *Lai Yunghai* of Nanjing University and members of the philosophy department of Chungshan University, Canton, for leading me to a Taoist recluse who dwells in a temple on a hilltop only a short walk into the fields behind Chungshan University. Taoist monks and nuns can be found on Ch'ing-ch'eng Shan near Chengtu city, Szechuan province, who spend most of their lives in *Ch'uan-chen* style Taoist meditation. The *Ch'uan-chen Chiao* ritual is performed by these Taoists only during the seventh and tenth months at the people's urging to "free souls" from the punishments of hell's alchemical furnace.

The practices of Taoist monastic life may on the surface seem to differ from those of the goal-oriented Black-head rites of the "fire-dwelling" household Taoists. In actuality, at the deeper, structural level the meditations of Taoist monks, nuns, and householders are analogous, if not identical. The Three Mountain Alliance Taoists of mainland and maritime China, though separated physically by mountain and ocean, are unified spiritually by the works of *Lao-tzu*, *Chuang-tzu*, the *Yellow Court Canon*, and the alchemical meditations of union with the *Tao*. Scholars and Western publishers who consider only the "etic" or surface level, *i.e.*, the observable aspects of the *Chiao*, while missing the meditative aspects of the *Lao-tzu* and inner alchemy, expound on only a portion of the Taoist tradition. Breath circulation, longevity practices, sexual hygiene, martial arts, and colorful *Chiao* liturgies are only an external and skillful means to care for the needs of the common folk.

China's popular festivals, the rites of passage, and the healing of social and physical ills are duties traditionally assigned by China's ancient culture to holy ascetics and mystics. Taoist priests, Buddhist monks, Christian ministers, and Muslim mullahs are expected to heal the sick, care for children, bless marriages and families, and bury the dead. The proper fulfillment of these duties requires that priests, monks, nuns, ministers, and mullahs be experts in self-discipline, prayer, and meditation before claiming to be a Taoist, Buddhist, or other religious expert. The Western use of Taoist techniques, such as breath exercises, martial arts, sex hygiene, and whatever else that has proved profitable in Western bookshops, often misses the point of true Taoist ascesis. To be truly Taoist, ascesis must be giving or emptying, not self-empowering.

To fill the self with power, glory, success, or wealth is to run contrary to the *Tao* of *Lao-tzu* and *Chuang-tzu*. To be filled with *Wu-wei* (the *Tao* of Transcendent Act) is to administer to all beings (the myriad creatures) with life-breath and healing (wholeness). The *Tao* gives primordial life-breath equally to all creatures.[39] Straw dogs, things cast aside, princes, and paupers are equally cared for and equally important to the meditating Taoist, who by internal emptying becomes one with the *Wu-wei Chih Tao* (the *Tao* of Transcendence). The *Chiao* rituals of the Three Mountain Alliance Taoists, found in Taiwan and mainland China, act out this meditative process of union.

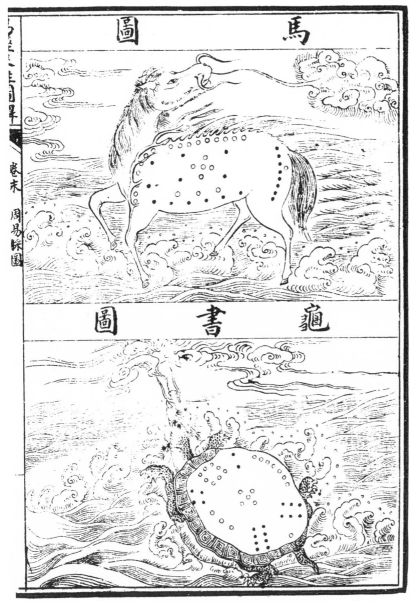

Ming dynasty woodblock print. (Top) The dragon-horse seen by *Fu Hsi* coming out of the Meng River, a tributary of the Yellow River, with the *Ho-t'u* depicted on the horse's back. Note that the artist has drawn the dots incorrectly. (Bottom) The mythical tortoise seen by *Yü* the Great coming out of the Lo River. The illustration is taken from the text of Lai Chih-te, *Lai Chu I-ching T'u Shuo*, p. 507.

Ming dynasty woodblock, an illustration from the *Jade Pivot Canon*. The meditation going on in the Taoist's mind during the performance of the *Chiao* ritual of cosmic renewal. The illustration shows the world of man below, and the Taoist traveling above to the heavens to an audience before the Primordial Heavenly Worthy.

Popular ritual in front of a local temple. The *Tang-ki* or medium cutting himself with a sword, while possessed by a spirit in trance. Note the *Fu* talisman dipped into the blood on his back.

The Taoist *Chuang-ch'en Teng-yün* poses in the *Pei-tou* or Pole-Star stance.

The laymen of the community enter the temple for morning ritual. In many parts of Taiwan the laymen dress in the robes of Ch'ing dynasty officials. Note that the three poles have been erected in front of the temple, signaling to the community of men and immortals that the *Chiao* festival of renewal has begun.

The *Fen Teng* ceremony of lighting the new fire, on the first evening of the *Chiao* festival. The second son of *Chuang-ch'en* (kneeling), the son chosen to succeed to the hereditary orthodox ordination, performs the rite, while his father, standing in the center, takes the role of the *Tu-chiang* or chief cantor.

A close-up of the *Tou* or bushel of rice, contributed by the *Ts-ai* family of Chung-kang ward, Chunan city, for the *Chiao* festival in the Matsu temple, December 1970. Note the swords, scale, scissors, and lantern put in the ornate wooden container, filled with rice.

The Taoist entourage, visiting one of the village families during the *Chiao*.

The *P'u-tu* banquet for the souls in hell, laid out on a table in front of a private residence. The figure of *Maitreya, Huan-hsi Fuo*, in the foreground shows the syncretistic nature of the Chinese religion. In front of the statue can be seen the family incense burner.

The Heavenly Master sect Red-head Taoist *Ch'ien Chih-ts'ai* (*Shen-hsiao* order), in full ceremonial dress. Note that the robes do not differ appreciably from those of the Black-head *Chuang-ch'en*. Ch'eng-huang temple, Hsinchu city, November 1964.

The author reading one of the canons of merit and repentance early in the morning of the second day of the *Chiao* festival of renewal. San-keng village, T'ao-yüan, November 1969.

The orthodox Heavenly Master sect Black-head Taoist (*Yü-fu* order) *Chuang-ch'en Teng-yün*, in full ceremonial robes. *Chiao* festival celebrated in Chunan city, the Matsu temple, December 1970.

# NOTES

## Introduction to the First Edition

1. *Chiao* means ritual sacrifice; Cf. Liu Chih-wan, *Taipei-shih Sung Shan Ch'i An Chien Chiao Chi Tien* (Nankang, Taipei: Academia Sinica Monograph 14, 1967), pp. 1-2.

2. Holmes Welch, *The Parting of the Way* (Boston: Beacon Press; London: Methuen & Co., Ltd. 1957), is the best popular source for the difference between philosophical and religious Taoism. Good reading and careful scholarship combine to make this a delightful book.

3. Henri Maspero, *Le Taoïsme*, in *Les Religions Chinoises*, vol. II (Paris: Musée Guimet, 1950).

4. Howard S. Levy, "Yellow Turban Religion and Rebellion at the End of the Han," *JOAS* 76, 4 (1956), pp. 214-227.

5. Ninji Ofuchi, *Dokyo-shi no Kenkyu* (University of Okayama: private publication, 1964). Ofuchi shows how the various practices of the Heavenly Master sect derive from Han dynasty village terms. Cf. also Rolf Stein, "Remarques sur les mouvements du Taoïsme politico-religieux au IIᵉ siècle après J. C.," in *T'oung Pao* 50 (1963), pp. 1-3.

6. The *Ling-pao* Taoists of Taiwan often include the word *Chi-chiu* in their title, whereas members of the orthodox Heavenly Master sect do not. The word was used from earliest times, that is, from the beginning of church Taoism during the Han period, to refer to the village Taoist.

7. The Heavenly Master was evicted from Lung-hu Shan in 1931 by the communist armies, and eventually came to Taiwan early in the nineteen-fifties. As 63rd-generation Heavenly Master, he was honored by the Nationalist government and made titular head of the Taoists on Taiwan. He recently died, and the 64th-generation Heavenly Master, a distant relative, was appointed to succeed him.

8. Ssu-ma Ch'ien, *Shih-chi*; P'an Ku, *Han Shu*; and *Yüeh Chüeh Shu* (The History of the Demise of the Kingdom of Yüeh) bear many passages relating to the ancestors of the Taoists, the court magicians and the *Fang-shih* of the early Han. *Han Wu-ti*, 140-86 B.C., was especially fond of bringing *Fang-shih* to court as favorites and then ordering their execution when their magic was inefficacious. The search for the mushrooms of longevity, appearance of spirits, and so forth typified court activities of the *Fang-shih*.

9. J. J. M. de Groot, *The Religious System of China*, 6 vols. (Leiden: E. J. Brill, 1892-1910). Cf. vol. 6.

10. The *Wei Shu* or *Apocrypha* are one of the richest sources of early Taoist ideas dating from the prior Han dynasty. The *Apocrypha* are a series of commentaries and descriptions of the *Ho-t'u* and the *Lo-shu*, two magical charts which are basic to Taoist liturgy. The *Chiang Hsiang* chapter of the *Apocrypha* identifies the *Ling-pao* Five Talismans used in Taoist liturgy with the *Ho-t'u*.

11. The *Wu Shang Pi Yao* section of the Taoist canon, vols. 768 to 779, dates from the sixth century A.D. Parts of the *Wu-shang Huang-lu Ta-chai*, a collection of Yellow Register rituals, can be dated to *Lu Hsiu-ching* in the Liang and the northern Wei periods, between 470 and 500 A.D. *Lu Hsiu-ching* died in 477, the historical accounts of his exploits showing that before his death he had collected the major texts used in the *Chiao* rituals much in their present-day form. Cf. Ch'en Kuo-fu, *Tao Tsang Yüan Liu K'ao* (Shanghai: Commercial Press, 1949), pp. 38-45.
12. Wei Po-yang, *Ts'an T'ung Ch'i*, Tao Tsang, vols. 621-629.
13. *Huang-t'ing Ching*, Tao Tsang, vols. 130-131; also vols. 189-190; 679.
14. Ko Hung, *Pao-p'u-tzu*, Tao Tsang, vols. 868-870; 871-873.
15. *Ta Tung Chen Ching*, Tao Tsang, vols. 16-17.
16. The summary here given was taken from the *Tao Chiao Yüan Liu* and the Ordination Manual of the Heavenly Master, *Chi Lu T'an Ch'ing Yüan K'o*, two unpublished manuscripts given by the Taoist *Chuang-ch'en* to the author.
17. The *Pa-ch'en T'u*, a part of a larger work called *Ch'i-men Tun-chia*, is a manual proper to the Wu-tang Shan sect from Hupei province, classified as the Pole Star Taoists. The *Ch'i-men Tun-chia* is a book of militaristic rituals which *Chu-ko Liang* was supposed to have used during the Three Kingdoms period to oppose the forces of *Ts'ao Ts'ao*. The *Pa-ch'en T'u* is based upon the eight trigrams of the *Lo-shu*, the diagrams used in the *Book of Changes*. On each of the points of the compass is a spirit, who can be summoned to win victory in military encounters. The book is thus associated with *Chu-ko Liang* and the Taoist monasteries of Shensi, Szechuan, and Hupei provinces dedicated to his honor.
18. Joseph Needham, *Science and Civilisation in China*, vol. II (Cambridge: Cambridge University Press, 1956), pp. 33-164; pp. 432-452.

# Chapter I

1. C. K. Yang, *Religion in Chinese Society* (Berkeley: University of California Press, 1961); Laurence G. Thompson, *Chinese Religion: An Introduction* (Belmont, California: Dickenson Publishing Company, 1969); De Groot, *The Religious System of China*.
2. *Tao Chiao Yüan Liu* (Taipei: Cheng-wen Publishing Co., in press).
3. Cf. Yu-lan Fung, *A History of Chinese Philosophy*, vols. 1 and 2; translated from the Chinese by Derk Bodde (Princeton: Princeton University Press, 1952-1953).
4. *Fan ken hui pen*, "restore the roots and return to the origin," a statement of the ends of interior meditation and of the ritual of orthodox Taoism.
5. *Tao Chiao Yüan Liu* (hereafter cited as *TCYL*), p. 89. See note 2 above.
6. *TCYL* p. 89; quoting the apocryphal commentary on the *I-ching, Ch'ien-tso T'u*.
7. *TCYL*, p. 83.
8. *TCYL*, p. 89; a direct quote from the *T'ai-chi T'u Shuo* of *Chou Tun-i*; p. 2., line 1.
9. *TCYL*, p. 90; a quote from *Huai-nan-tzu*, p. 7, p. 2b, line 10.
10. *TCYL*, p. 83, lines 7-8; *Huai-nan-tzu*, ch. 7, p. 3b, line 2.
11. De Groot, vol. 4, p. 3.
12. *Ibid.*, vol. 4, p. 5. Cf. *Li Chi*, Kuo-chi ed., vol. 92, Shang p. 64.
13. *Ibid.*, vol. 4, p. 4. *Li Chi*, Kuo-chi ed., vol. 93, p. 55.
14. Folk tale taken from Masuda Fukutaro, *Taiwan no Shukyo* (The Religions of Taiwan), pp. 26-27.
15. The ritual of expelling the boats of pestilence is quite popular, especially in southern and central Taiwan. It belongs to the kinds of ritual performed by the Red-head *Lü Shan* Taoists.
16. *Yu-ying Kung*, the orphan souls and their temples are well-known phenomena throughout Taiwan. Cf. Masuda Fukutaro, *Taiwan no Shukyo*, pp. 35-36.
17. De Groot, vol. 4, pp. 5-30.
18. Cf. the *Su Ch'i* ritual, as explained in ch. 4.

19. At the *Chiao* festival, the leading families contribute the most money and are given the favored places in the procession for floating the lanterns.

20. A medium, the man or woman possessed of a demon, and the shaman, who travels to the heavens to stand before the gods, are to be distinguished in the Chinese religion into two different categories. The *Tang-ki*, who is possessed and speaks in the voice of the spirit, is perhaps better defined as a medium. The Taoist, who travels before the Heavenly Worthies in the Prior Heavens during his ritual meditations, might perhaps be termed a shaman-priest.

21. The Taoist's robes symbolize a heavenly mandarin. The nine grades of ordination imitate the ranks of the imperial mandarinate.

22. *Taiwan Sheng T'ung Chih Kao* (Taiwan Provincial Gazette); *Tsung-chiao P'ien Chuan Erh*, Section on Religions, vol. 2 (Taipei: Taiwan Wenhsien Wei-yüan Hui, 1956).

23. Cheng Sheng-ch'ang, *Shen-ming Lai Li chi Nien Chieh Yu-lai* (The Historical Origins of the Spirits and Festivals [of Taiwan]) (Changhua: Yang Kuang press, 1967).

24. Thompson, *Chinese Religion*, pp. 29-30, quotes Burkhardt's *Chinese Creeds and Customs* showing how symbols of *Yang* are used in rites of exorcism to expel evil demons. The preliminaries to the New Year festival are in fact purificatory-exorcist in nature, and are similar to the month-long preparations which precede the *Chiao* festival of renewal.

25. The arrival of the heavenly spirits and the end of the banquet, *i.e.*, when the spirits have eaten their fill, is determined by casting the fortune blocks, called "*Boa-poe*" in Amoy dialect. The fortune blocks are quarter-moon-shaped, wooden blocks, one side rounded off to represent *Yang*, and the other side smooth and flat to represent *Yin*. When the blocks fall with *Yang* and *Yin* balanced, that is with round side and flat side showing three times in a row, the spirits are considered to have given a "yes" answer. Two flat sides (*Yin*) is a "no," two round sides (*Yang*) means "the gods are laughing."

26. Cf. Cheng, pp. 16-20. The author has heard this story in the Ch'ing-shui Tsu-shih temple of Tamshui city, near Taipei. Cf. also Masuda Fukutaro, pp. 36-37.

27. The offering of the turtle cakes in honor of the spirit of the soil can be seen in many of the temples of Taipei city throughout the entire second lunar month. The shrine to the spirit of the soil located at Roosevelt Road, section 3, lane 202, sponsors a month-long series of popular operas and puppet shows which last through most of the night, and can be heard as far away as the campus of Taiwan University. On each day of the public performances, a different family offers a large, decorated cake, shaped like a turtle with the characters "longevity," "wealth," and "blessing" written on top. Most temples simply offer the round, flat, steamed breads with red food coloring on the exterior, which are also called "turtle cakes" and are offered for the same purpose.

28. This and the following sets of stories or hagiographies of the spirits are taken from Cheng's *Shen-ming Lai-li*, unless otherwise specified.

29. Masuda Fukutaro, pp. 29-31.

30. In many parts of China the cold-food festival is celebrated on the same day as the *Ch'ing Ming* festival, 105 days after the winter solstice.

31. Cf. *Tao Tsang* (Taoist Canon) vol. 580, ch. 1, p. 25, a picture of a Taoist priest sitting atop a slain tiger. From the top of the Taoist's head issues a cloud of vapor, in the center of which can be seen the Three Pure Ones. Above the Taoist's head is the moon on the right and the sun on the left, symbols of *Yin* and *Yang*. The slain tiger is symbolic of *Yin* under control.

32. *Wei Shu*, Apocrypha, ch. 32, *Ho-t'u Chiang Hsiang*, the "coming down" or revelation of the symbols called *Ho-t'u*; the gloss to the text quotes the *Yüeh Chüeh Shu*, The History of the Fall of the Kingdom of *Yüeh*, saying that the *Ling-pao* Five Talismans, the *Ho-t'u* revealed to *Yü* the Great, were buried by *Yü* atop Pao Shan (in the Mao Shan complex near Nanjing) after he had used them to control the floods. Cf. Mo-hai Chin-hu edition, vol. 8, pp. 4603-4604.

33. There are many Taoist rituals or occasions for liturgical celebration called *Chiao*. The expulsion of the demons of pestilence, avoidance of calamity of any sort, and funeral ritual are all based on the same liturgical principle used in the *Chiao*. The so-called *Ch'ing Chiao*, the "Pure" *Chiao*, and the *Chiao* of dedication for a temple are the specific rituals described here. They occur most frequently during the eleventh and twelfth lunar months.

# Chapter II

1. The method of prognostication by using the fortune blocks, as described in chapter 1, note 25, is used to determine what year and what month and day the temple should be rededicated through a *Chiao* festival of renewal. Ideally the sixty-year *Chia-tzu* cycle should be completed, but in fact the *Chiao* can occur as often as the temple needs repairs, and money for the expensive celebration can be accumulated.
2. Cf. illustration in photo section for the *Tou* bushel of rice and its contents.
3. The articles listed are associated with *Yin*, death, and impurity.
4. No matter in which direction a temple faces in actuality, the entrance of the temple is ritually considered to be the south, the place from which the people worship. The west side, that is, the wall on the left as one enters the temple, is the *Yin* part, and the east side is the *Yang* area. The back of the temple, where the tutelary deities are housed and honored, is the north, the place in which the emperor sits in the imperial courtrooms. During the *Chiao* rituals of renewal, the north wall of the temple is dedicated to the Taoist's spirits from the Prior Heavens, and a table near the south side, the temple's main entrance, seats the patron spirits of the Chinese religion.
5. The temporary structures erected in the plazas around the city are properly speaking called *Muo* or tents, lodgings for the deities of the popular religion who are invited to be present. There were twenty-three such structures erected in Chunan, in December, 1970, one for each of the city's leading families. The word *T'an* or "Altar" is given to the colorful structures by the people of north Taiwan.
6. Liu Chih-wan, *Taipei-shih Sung-shan Ch'i An Chien Chiao Chi Tien* (Great Rites of Propitiation at Sung-shan) (Taipei: Academia Sinica Monograph 14, Nan-kang, Taipei, 1967).
7. Cf. Ofuchi Ninji, *Dokyo Shi no Kenkyu* (Studies on the History of Taoism) (Okayama: Okayama Daigaku, 1964), p. 183; Rolf Stein, "Remarques sur les mouvements politico-religieux au II$^c$ siècle après J.C." *T'oung Pao*, vol. 50 (1963), pp. 1-76, for similarity in Han village usage and Taoist titles.
8. Wolfram Eberhard, *Guilt and Sin in Traditional China* (Berkeley: University of California Press, 1967), p. 12.
9. Eberhard, pp. 46-55.
10. Cf. Tseng Ching-lai, *Taiwan Shukyo to Meishin Roshu* (Taiwanese Religion and Rigid Superstitions) (Society for the Study of Taiwanese Religions, 1938), pp. 87-116, for a treatise on the orphan souls and their cult in the *Yu-ying Kung* temples of Taiwan.
11. Carl F. Kupfer, *Sacred Places in China* (Cincinnati: Western Methodist Book Concern Press, 1911), pp. 92-106, for photos and description of Lung-hu Shan and Ch'ing-chou village. The 62nd-generation Heavenly Master is shown with his two wives and children.
12. The word *K'o-i*, literally "alternating ritual," is used in Buddhist monasteries to refer to the public debate between two masters. In the Taoist sense it refers to the liturgy of dialogue between the two principles *Yang* and *Yin*. The chief cantor, *Tu-chiang*, stands to the east side of the central altar, singing the role of *Yang*, and sounding the brass gong. The assistant cantor, *Fu-chiang*, stands on the west side of the altar, singing the role of *Yin*, and striking the wooden fish, *Mu-yü*. The high priest, *Kao-kung Fa-shih*, fulfills the role of the *T'ai-chi*, the Great Ultimate. He stands in the center of the cosmos and meditates.
13. Cf. ch. 4, where the lists of Buddhist and Taoist canons appear to be quite similar. One might surmise that the development of the Taoist canons of merit and repentance were

historically conceived as a counter-measure to the popular Buddhist Mahayana canons. Cf. Fukui Kojun, *Dokyo no Kiso teki Kenkyu* (A Basic Study of Religious Taoism) (Tokyo: Shoseki Bunbutsu Ryutsu kai, 1952), ch. 1, pp. 92-131.

14. In Buddhist terminology *Tao Ch'ang* means *Bodhimandala*, the circle or place in which the enlightenment of the *Buddha* took place. By derived meaning it is a place or method for deriving Buddhist truth, or simply a place for teaching, learning, or practicing religion. Cf. William Soothill, *A Dictionary of Chinese Buddhist Terms* (London: Kegan Paul, Trench, Trubner & Co.; Taipei: Cheng-wen Publishing Co., 1969), p. 416. To the Taoist, *Tao Ch'ang* refers to the ritual celebrating a banquet of the Three Pure Ones in the center of the cosmos, the "Yellow Court of Center," with the series of rituals listed here under numbers 2, 3, and 4.

# Chapter III

1. The translation of the *Huai-nan-tzu* consists of introductory passages from the first, third, and seventh chapters. The version is a free rather than a literal translation, based on the notes of the commercial press edition, *Kuo Hsüeh Chi-pen* series, *Liu Wen-tien* commentary and text.

2. Taoist canon vol. 563, ch. 2, pp. 12-14.

3. The original *Ho-t'u*, prior to the *Wei Shu* Apocryphal texts, had little or nothing to do with the later systematization of the *Yin-yang* five-element theory described here. Early accounts describe the *Ho-t'u* as precious stones, perhaps made of jade, which were used as a *Pao*, *i.e.*, talismanic objects winning blessing from heaven. There was probably no relationship between the original *Ho-t'u* and the *Lo-shu*, though the unknown writers of the Apocryphal texts had already begun associating the two charts with each other. A gloss in the *Ho-t'u* section of the Apocrypha identifies the *Ling-pao* Five Talismans with a *Ho-t'u*. That the *Ho-t'u* is to be identified with the *Chia-tzu* heavenly spirits as listed here can be seen from the Apocryphal books *Wei Shu*, the various chapters describing the composition of the *Ho-t'u*; Cf. *Muo-hai Chin-shu*, vols. 7 and 8; *i.e.*, *Wei Shu* commentaries on the *Book of History, Book of Odes*, and the *Ho-t'u*. The association of the five spirits, five directions, and so forth, with vapors which fill the five organs, is to be found in the *Pao-p'u-tzu*, ch. 15, p. 8a, lines 8-10. The passage in the *Pao-p'u-tzu* describes how the Taoist implants the colored vapors of the five elements into the corresponding organs of the body during meditation. The association of the numbers as listed here with the *Ho-t'u* is to be found in the *Hsi-tz'u* appendix of the *I-ching*, ch. 3.

4. The chart is also found in Liu I-ming, *I-tao Hsin-fa Chen Chuan* (Shensi: Chi-yün Monastery, 1799); the text was reprinted by the Tzu-yu press in Taipei in 1962, p. 1.

5. Lai Chih-te, *Lai Chu I-ching T'u-chieh* (Ming woodblock print, 1568); Taipei reprint, I-chün Press, 1969, p. 23.

6. Cf. note 32, ch. 1. The identification of the *Ho-t'u* with the *Ling-pao* Five Talismans is to be found in the little-known *Wei Shu* Apocrypha, the chapter describing the *Ho-t'u*, called *Chiang-hsiang*, the "Revelation of the Ho-t'u." The gloss to the text quotes the *Yüeh Chüeh Shu*, the account of *Yü* the Great who controlled the floods by using *Ling-pao* Five Talismans, a kind of *Ho-t'u* revealed by a spirit. When he had finished using them, he buried the talismans in a spirit-cave in the Mao Shan range. The *Ling-pao* Five Talismans are but one type of *Ho-t'u*, however; the use of the chart in geomancy and in the *I-ching* is not in the minds of the users to be associated with the highly secret and esoteric rite called *Su Ch'i* when the Five Talismans (the *Ling-pao* Five Talismans) are planted by ritual meditation into the cosmos. See the *I-tao Hsin-fa*, as in note 5 above, pp. 1-34.

7. *I-tao Hsin-fa*, pp. 6-8. The explanation of the *Ho-t'u* as described here was given orally to the author by the Taoist *Chuang-ch'en*, whose ritual will be described in the following chapter. The *I-tao Hsin-fa* was later purchased by the author in a Taipei bookstall, when *Chuang* found it on the shelf and recommended the book as the proper explanation for

instructions to precede ritual meditation. Note that the term *Ch'ang-sheng* means not only "longevity" but also "continuing birth"; that is, with *Yang* and *Yin* always together, as in the *Ho-t'u*, there is continual birth.

8. That is, the *Su Ch'i* ritual at midnight after the first full day of ritual, when the *Ho-t'u* is implanted in the microcosm, the Morning, Noon and Night Audiences of the second day, a "joining of the Three Fives"; and, finally, the *Tao-ch'ang* on the third day, a banquet for the eternal aspect of the *Tao* in the center of the cosmos, thus winning "eternal life," or "eternal birth."

9. *I-tao Hsin-fa*, pp. 5, 26.

10. *I-tao Hsin-fa*, p. 20.

11. Cf. *Lai Chu I-ching T'u-Chieh*, as in note 6, above, pp. 507-520, for the various symbolization attributed to the *Lo-shu*.

12. Cf. vol. 985 of the Taoist canon, the rubrical description of the *Chin T'an* ritual, for the various forms of the steps of *Yü*.

# Chapter IV

1. There are many kinds of *Chiao* festivals, celebrated at other times of the year. The *Ch'ing Chiao*, that is, the "Pure" festival of renewal, is usually celebrated during the eleventh or twelfth month, around the time of the winter solstice. The *Chiao* for expelling the demons of pestilence is more frequently celebrated during the summer months, around the time of the summer solstice.

2. There is certainly some levity associated with the practice of taking the food offerings off the altar, which were put there by the pious faithful, and eating them noticed or unnoticed by the donor. *Chuang-ch'en* forbids all levity and does not allow the food or wine on the altar to be touched. But the author has also seen Taoists take bottles of rice wine off the sacrificial altars and enjoy a drink during the dinner or supper served between ceremonies. The devout laymen at least tolerate the Taoists who feel it their privilege to partake of the food offerings.

3. The *Chiao* usually lasts only three or five days in modern-day Taiwan. Chinese from the mainland who lived near Taoist centers have described to the author continuing forty-nine- and ninety-nine-day *Chiao* performed in the Mao Shan monastery near Nanjing, and the Hua Shan monastery near Sian in Shensi. The Taoists of Taiwan speak of the longer *Chiao* ritual, and some boast that they can perform the longer nine-day variety, making use of many more canonical readings and texts. The basic rituals of the *Chiao*, however, remain the same, that is, those described below for the three-day *Chiao*, excluding the canons of merit and repentance, which can be multiplied or shortened at will. The cost of the *Chiao* is, undoubtedly, one of the main factors in limiting the festivities to three or five days.

4. The versions of the rituals in the Taoist canon are not complete. One must make use of the secret manuals given to the young Taoist by his master or his father at the time of ordination to understand the totality of the ritual. The Taoist canon has only the bare skeleton of the liturgy, perhaps one third of what the Taoist must know in order to perform the rites efficaciously. The manuals and documents of the Taoists of Taiwan are, therefore, invaluable material for interpreting the meaning of the Taoist canon.

5. In each of the Taoist sects, there are nine grades of excellence, determined by the Taoist's knowledge of rituals and ability to summon spirits. A grade-six Taoist is one who knows how to *Ch'u Kuan*, that is, how to "summon forth" the spirits of the Prior Heavens to effect cosmic renewal. The ritual of ordination and the knowledge of the spirits is considered to be the special prerogative of the Heavenly Master at Lung-hu Shan. Thus every Taoist, no matter what his rank or ability, owes allegiance to the Heavenly Master, the successor of *Chang Tao-ling*, the founder of the order, to whom was revealed in vision the rite called *Ch'u-Kuan*, "Exteriorizing and Commanding the Spirits."

6. Cf. Taoist canon, vol. 975, ch. 8, pp. 30-30b, for a woodblock print of the old Taoist *T'an* shaped like a square. Note that the eight trigrams of King *Wen*, that is, the *Lo-shu*, are depicted as making up the central section of the *T'an*. The shape of the altar can be dated to the early Han period, and the cult of *T'ai-i* set up by *Han Wu-ti*, on the model of the *Lo-shu*.

7. It has been suggested by some researchers on Taiwan that there are as many poles as there are days to the *Chiao* ritual. Whatever the origin of this belief, the cities and villages of North Taiwan consistently erect only three poles for a three- or five-day *Chiao*, as described here. The author has seen both three- and five-day *Chiao* festivals with only three poles, and has heard of three-day *Chiao* festivals with as many as six poles, representing more spirits than those listed in this chapter. Many of the townships in southern Taiwan erect a pole in front of every family which takes part in the *Chiao*. Illustrations in the Taoist canon often show a pole and a lantern for every spirit that has been invited. Whatever the custom of former days and other places, the practice of the people of north Taiwan is to limit the poles to three, as far as the author can see from his own field experience. Liu chin-wan, *op. cit.*, reports six poles in the *Chiao* celebrated at Sung-shan, Taipei.

8. Taoist canon, vol. 985, Lü T'ai-ku, *Chin T'an*, ch. 7.

9. Throughout the following pages, the spirits, vapors, and mythical animals described are seen only by the chief Taoist and by his disciples, through the meditations going on within the mind during the ritual. The Taoist sees the dragon, the phoenix, and so forth, in his imagination. The devout members of the community see only the external ritual, the frenzied dance steps, and the various purifications. Taoist canon, vol. 985, ch. 7, p. 2, line 8.

10. *Ibid.*, p. 2b.

11. *Ibid.*, p. 3, lines 4-10. The Taiwanese Taoist's version does not differ substantially from the canonical version. The Taiwan version names the orifices through which the mythical animals emerge from the microcosm. The dragon comes forth through the left eye; the tiger from the right nostril; the phoenix comes through the mouth; the tortoise comes through the ears. The Taiwanese text thus completes the canonical version, showing how macrocosm and microcosm correspond in the mind of the Taoist.

12. *Ibid.*, p. 3b, lines 4-5.

13. *Ibid.*, lines 8-10.

14. *Ibid.*, p. 4, lines 6-7. The canonical version is corrupt here; the Taiwanese text is in strict classical verse.

15. *Ibid.*, p. 7, line 5 to p. 7b, line 1.

16. The similarity between this passage and the spirits of the *Ho-t'u*, mentioned in chapter three, is perhaps obvious; the numbers 9 for east, 3 for south, 7 for west, and 5 for the north do not correspond to the commonly known *Ho-t'u* (5 in the center) but to the secret esoteric symbol, the *Ling-pao* Five Talismans of the Taoist. The same series of numbers will be used in the *Su Ch'i* ritual of renewal to symbolize the life-bearing spirits of the Prior Heavens.

17. *Ibid.*, p. 8, line 8.

18. *Ibid.*, p. 9, line 1.

19. *Ibid.*, p. 9, lines 5-7.

20. *Ibid.*, p. 9b, lines 4-10.

21. Taoist canon, vol. 958, ch. 7, p. 10, lines 5-10; compare the *Huang-t'ing Wai-ching Hsia* (part 3) pp. 6-6b, and the *Huang-T'ing Nei Ching*, Tzu-yu press edition, pp. 34-35.

22. The passages from the *Huang-t'ing Ching* (*Yellow Court Canon*) are missing from the texts used by the lower-grade Taoists of Taiwan. A Taoist's rank is determined by the spirits he can summon; the highest-ranking Taoist is one who knows the spirits and meditations of the *Yellow Court Canon*, that is, the *Mao Shan* tradition. Knowledge of these spirits and their use in ritual meditation therefore indicate that the Taoist's family line received a very high ordination sometime in its history, even if the Taoist in the present generation does not bear a high-ranking title. A ranking title, however, without the requisite knowledge,

can be immediately detected by the Taoist. Jealous preservation of one's powers and secrets is, therefore, almost an endemic condition for the Taiwanese Taoists, who are most unwilling to talk of their lists of spirits and other trade secrets, or to allow their ritual manuals to be seen by others.

23. Taoist canon, vol. 985, ch. 7, p. 12b, lines 8-10. The word *Chen* or "true" is here to be rendered "realized," in the sense that the ultimate *Tao* of transcendence, the *Wu-chi*, will be present in the center of the microcosm only when the whole body has been totally purified from the forces of *Yin*; "realization," enlightenment, and the presence of the eternal *Tao* are thus equivalent.

24. The rubrics are found in vol. 985, ch. 7, pp. 13-13b, with illustrations, as here depicted. The same rubrics are performed by the Taoists of Taiwan at the beginning of every temple ritual, as a preliminary step to orthodox liturgy.

25. Thus the purpose of Taoist liturgy is seen in a clearer light; the meditations of inner alchemy, whereby the body is purified, organ by organ, are here accomplished through an audience of the spirits in the body with the eternal transcendent *Tao* in the Yellow Court of the center, *i.e.*, the center of the microcosm. The organs are each conceived of as being the dwelling place of a spirit or spirits. The spirits are summoned forth from the microcosm for the audience with the *Tao*. The very presence of the eternal *Tao*, due to the sacramental powers of the Taoist for purification of the microcosm and subsequently summoning forth of the spirits, is efficacious enough to win rebirth, renewal, and eternal life. The theme is, however, not explained to the laity; it is an interpretation of the *Yellow Court Canon*, as the basis for Taoist liturgical meditation, given to the author by *Chuang-ch'en*, and taught to his disciples for the performance of liturgy.

26. The texts mentioned here can all be found in the Taoist canon; Cf. Three Officials canon, vol. 295, Pole Star canon, vol. 341, Southern Star canon, vol. 341, the Jade Pivot canon, vol. 25, and the canons of the Three Origins, vol. 295. A woodblock print showing the meditation going on within the mind of the Taoist while reading the Jade Pivot canon appears in the photo section.

27. The Noon Offering, also called Sacrificial Offering (*Wu Hsien* or *Hung Hsien*), can be found in the Taoist canon, vol. 564.

28. The *Fen Teng* is found partially in the Taoist canon, vol. 213, ch. 27. The complete text as used by the Taoists of Taiwan and of Fukien province can be found in the British Museum in manuscript form under the catalogue number OR 12693/28. The text is identical with that used by the Taoists of Taiwan, and will be used as a reference for the quotations in the following pages. The passage here quoted is from pp. 3-7 of the British Museum copy.

29. *Fen Teng*, p. 8.

30. The rubrics described here are not performed by most of the Taoists of Taiwan; they were learned by the grandfather of *Chuang-ch'en* while at Lung-hu Shan in 1859, and performed only by the entourage of disciples as trained by *Chuang* himself. Variations on ritual performance are to be found with each of the Taoist groups throughout Taiwan, emphasizing both the different sources for Taoist ritual and the corrupting influence of the *Lü Shan* Taoists in the rituals of the Red-head or *Shen-hsiao* order. Just as Chinese religion is rich in local practices, differing for every district within China, so, too, the Taoists vary the details of ritual performance according to their source of origin and the various sects within Taoist ranks.

31. *Chuan Lien*, "Rolling up the Screen," is to be found in the Taoist canon, vol. 212, ch. 17. The British Museum manuscript OR 12693/28 (p. 10), from Changchou city in Fukien, presents the rite immediately after the *Fen Teng* ceremony.

32. Taoist canon, vol. 211, ch. 14, *Ming Chung Chia Ch'ing*, "Sounding the Brass Bowl and the Stone Chime"; British Museum copy, OR 12693/28, beginning on p. 28.

33. Cf. Taoist canon, vol. 281, ch. 16, *Su Ch'i*.

34. Taken from *I-tao Hsin-fa* pp. 6-7. The illustration is from a publication by a group of Taoist laymen centered in Taipei who claim allegiance to the *Lung-men* sect, called *Chin-tan Ta Ch'eng Chi*, "A Collection of Writings on the Formation of the Golden Pill of Immortality." The quote is from the *Ts'an T'ung Ch'i Hsia* (part 3), p. 57, and from the *Huang-t'ing Ching*, exterior section (*Huang-t'ing Wai-ching*), Chung (part two), p. 3, lines 4-6.

35. The meditation of the Morning Audience is described in the Taoist canon, vol. 967, ch. 21, p. 6, lines 7-10. The text for the Morning Audience is in vol. 282, ch. 17. Without the prompt books and explanations of the Taoists of Taiwan, it would be impossible to know from the text in vol. 282 the meditation which the high priest performs.

36. Taoist canon, vol. 967, ch. 21, p. 8, lines 1-2.

37. Taoist canon, vol. 967, ch. 21, p. 8, lines 5 and following.

38. The high priest performs at this time a meditation which is the reverse of the *Su Ch'i* performed at midnight the first evening of the *Chiao* rituals. The five True Writs, which were "planted" during the *Su Ch'i*, are now "harvested" (*Shou Chen-wen*), or restored to their original positions within the microcosm of the Taoist's body, and in the stars of the Prior Heavens. The *T'an* or sacred temple area is now dismantled in the Taoist's mind, after which time the offering of less pure foods, raw meat for the demons and cooked meat for human beings and spririts, is permitted.

# Chapter V

1. This is a rewrite of chapter five from the first edition, with an update of Taoism as practiced on the China mainland up to the time of this second printing in 1989. My surveys of Taoism in the People's Republic of China and other recent studies of Taoism have spurred the revision of this section.

2. See Ch'en Kuo-fu, *Tao Tsang Yüan Liu K'ao*, 2 vols. (Peking: Chung Hua Press, 1963) for a division of religious Taoism according to the formation of the Taoist canon.

3. Yoshioka Yoshitoyo, *Eisei e no Negai* (Tokyo: Tankosha, 1970), pp. 248-259; also Kubo Noritada, *Dokyo Shi* (Tokyo: Yamakawa Shuppansha, 1977), pp. 8-20.

4. The pioneer work of Kristofer M. Schipper, who delivered an unpublished mimeographed paper entitled "Taoism: The Liturgical Tradition" at the First International Conference on Religious Taoism, Bellagio, Italy, in 1968, brought attention to the existence of *Ling-pao* liturgy as practiced by the *Ch'en* family in Tainan city, south Taiwan. *Meng-wei* Taoism, as practiced by the *Cheng-i Szu-t'an* of Hsinchu city, north Taiwan, is externally similar, but internally, *i.e.*, at the meditative level, is quite distinct from the Tainan practices.

5. John Lagerwey, *Taoist Ritual in Chinese Society and History* (New York and London: MacMillan, 1987); and Ofuchi Ninji, *Chugokujin no Shukyo Girei* (Tokyo: Fukutake Shoten, 1983).

6. Field notes of the author, Changchou city, July 1988. John Lagerwey (Paris) and Kenneth Dean (Stanford) also have studied the Taoists of south Fukien; their surveys are forthcoming in *Cahiers d'Extreme Asie*, vol. 4, and "The Study of Taoist Ritual Music," (Chinese University, Hong Kong) respectively.

7. See Michael Saso, *Chuang-lin Hsü Tao-tsang* (Taipei: Cheng-wen Press, 1975) vols. 20-25, for a discussion of the *Shen-hsiao* Red-head style of *Chiao*.

8. The *Shen-hsiao* style liturgy, its origins, and presence in modern Taiwan are discussed in a balanced, scholarly treatment by Judith Boltz, *A Survey of Taoist Literature* (Berkeley: University of California, 1987), pp. 26-29, and passim. Though no Taoists now call themselves *Shen-hsiao*, the style of liturgy used by some Red-heads is identified by that title. Black-head Taoists of the *Cheng-i Szu-t'an* of north Taiwan name the texts used in these liturgies as *Shen-hsiao* style, as do the masters of Lung-hu Shan in Kiangsi province.

9. Note that the Red-head *Ling-pao* Taoists of Changchou city, who belong to the *Liu* clan and their entourage, do use the *An Chen-wen* and *Shou Chen-wen* rites in the liturgies called *Su-ch'i* and *Tao ch'ang* as described in chapter four. The texts are identical with those used

by the Black-head Taoists of north Taiwan, and the *Cheng-i Meng-wei* Taoists of Lung-hu Shan, San-ch'ing Kung, in Kiangsi.

10. The *Fa-lu* rite is described and translated in Michael Saso, *The Teachings of Taoist Master Chuang* (New Haven: Yale University Press, 1978), pp. 225-233. Note the difference in this *Meng-wei* version of the ritual meditation and that of Ofuchi, Lagerwey, and Schipper: John Lagerwey, *Taoist Ritual in Chinese Society and History* (New York and London: MacMillan, 1987), pp. 122-123. Taoists of the *Meng-wei* and *Shang-ch'ing* tradition use the *Fa-lu* rite to empty the microcosm of spirits before union with the *Tao*, *i.e.*, as a meditation of kenosis-like emptying. Taoists of the *Ling-pao* and popular traditions simply use the *Fa-lu* to summon spirits.

11. From the Sui through the T'ang period, 581-907 A.D., *Shang-ch'ing*, *Ling-pao*, and *Cheng-i Meng-wei* registers were ranked first, second, and third in that order. From the Sung-Yüan dynasties onward, the *Cheng-i Meng-wei* register was given second and *Ling-pao* a lower rank. See note 13, below.

12. See Michael Saso, *Dokyo Hiketsu Shusei* (Tokyo: Ryukei Shosha, 1978-1979), p. 32. The author's visits to Lung-hu Shan, Mao Shan, and Wu-tang Shan in 1987-1988 revealed that they recognized the Three Mountain Alliance and transmit registers to young Taoists in accordance with tradition. Professor *Ch'en Ta-ts'an* of the Shanghai Conservatory of Music reports that such activities at Ko-tsao Shan had not yet been restored as of 1987.

13. A forty-character poem is used by members of the alliance to identify the recipient of registers and ordination, generation by generation. *I.e.*, the next character in line is assigned to the generation of disciples beneath the Taoist master who received the license to perform liturgy. Taoists of Hsinchu, Shanghai, Suchow, Mao Shan, and Lung-hu Shan at present use the twenty-eighth, twenty-ninth, and thirtieth generation characters, suggesting a Sung dynasty origin for the alliance. Red-head Taoists of the *Lin* clan lineage, on the other hand, use a variant reading of the poem and do not strictly follow the "once a generation" rule. All Taoists are required to sign their *Lu* register and their identifying character from the poem to all liturgical documents used during a ritual. The scholar can identify the grade, rank, and generation of the Taoist by reading these ritual documents, which are meant to be read and burned during liturgies.

14. This title (Three Arcana Five Thunder Registers and Canons) distinguishes these registers of the Three Mountain Alliance from those of the popular Five Thunder Magic of the *Shen-hsiao*, *Lü Shan*, and other Taoists found in Taiwan, Fukien, and Kwangtung. Taoist oral tradition of the *Cheng-i Szu t'an* of north Taiwan, Mao Shan in Kiangsu, and Master *Wang Shao-lin* of Lung-hu Shan confirm the distinction. The registers are identified with the *Ch'ing-wei* tradition, attributed to a lady Taoist, *Tsu Shu* (ca. 889-904 A.D.). See Judith Boltz, *A Survey of Taoist Literature* (Berkeley: University of California, 1987), pp. 39-41, 68-70.

15. See *Tao-tsang* TTHY #1199, 1200, Fascicles 877-878 in the 1923 Commercial Press edition, Shanghai, 1923-1924.

16. See Lagerwey and Ofuchi, cited in note 5, above. Further investigation will prove, I am sure, that the Tainan Taoists also know the meditations of internal alchemy, a topic which the Taoist masters are forbidden to speak about unless the scholar has received initiation of some sort into Taoist prayer.

17. See Michael Saso, "Religion in the People's Republic," *China News Analysis*, Hong Kong, December 15, 1987.

18. The content of the registers coincide with the *Hua Shan Mi-chüeh* and the *Nei-wai T'ien-kang Chüeh* manuals listed on p. 300 of Michael Saso, *The Teachings of Taoist Master Chuang* (New Haven: Yale University Press, 1978). I was able to go over these manuals word-by-word with Master *Shih* and watch his performance of the various steps of *Yü*, the circulation of inner breath, and visualization of the Pole Star and Thunder spirits.

19. See Judith Boltz, *A Survey of Taoist Literature* (Berkeley: University of California, 1987), pp. 119-121 for the relationship of Wu-tang Shan with Thunder and Pole Star ritual. The

journey on the Yangtze River ferry from Shanghai and Nanjing is a three- to four-day trip to Wuhan, from whence one takes the Szechuan line train, overnight on a hard seat, to Shih-yen city. Arriving early in the morning, the traveler must transfer to a bus for a six-hour ride to Wu-tang Shan hostel, then a three-hour walk to the summit. The visitor can stay overnight in public hostels and lunch with the Taoists.

20. A tree planted by *Sung Kao-tsung* in 1129 A.D. stands in the temple courtyard. The original buildings were left intact by the Red Guard. However, they destroyed the statues before restraint was imposed.

21. Michael Saso, *The Teachings of Taoist Master Chuang* (New Haven: Yale University Press, 1978), pp. 300, and 281, n. 156.

22. The *Tao-chiao Yüan-liu*, which is found in many local Taoist collections, is partially published in Michael Saso, *Chuang-lin Hsü Tao-tsang* (Taipei: Cheng-wen Press, 1975), vol. 19, the *Wen-chien* collection. The list repeated here is found in Michael Saso, *Dokyo Hiketsu Shusei* (Tokyo: Ryukei Shosha, 1978-1979), pp. 6-7.

23. My former writings are inaccurate on this point. *T'ien-shu* can refer to the *Ch'ing-wei* Thunder registers of the second and third Mao Shan peaks, according to the recent *Mao Shan T'ung-chih* and the oral accounts of the Taoist masters now living there. A brief history of the *Ch'ing-wei* order and its Thunder ritual is found in Boltz, pp. 38-40. It also seems to be used by other monastic orders, but not the Thunder magic of the *Shen-hsiao* and other popular sects.

24. The term *Yü-fu* (Jade Prefecture) is the name of a monastic complex at Mao Shan where *Cheng-i, Ling-pao*, and other forms of canonical ritual are practiced. Master *Shih* at Mao Shan, as well as *Wang Shao-lin* at Lung-hu Shan, recognize this title.

25. See Michael Saso, *Chuang-lin Hsü Tao-tsang* (Taipei: Cheng-wen Press, 1975) vols. 20-25, for this style of liturgy.

26. The *Chiao* ritual performed by Master *Liu* has been studied and video-recorded by Kenneth Dean and reported on by John Lagerwey in forthcoming publications: see *Cahiers d'Extreme Asie*, vols. 3-4 (Kyoto), and the "Conference Papers on Taoist Liturgical Music," Chinese University, Hong Kong.

27. A complete set of *Chiao* ritual manuals has not yet been restored to the twenty or more Taoists who work in the greater Chuanchou area. The *Ch'en* clan, with the support of the Religious Affairs Bureau and the Kuan-kung temple, is in the process of finding and restoring classical *Cheng-i* rites and materials preserved in Changchou city and Taiwan.

28. John Lagerwey in personal communication with the author noted that Red-head Taoists do not observe this rule, *i.e.*, the use of the character does not represent a specific generation, but is changed each time the register is passed on to a disciple. In my recent survey of mainland Taoists, however, it seems certain that the Three Mountain Drop of Blood Alliance does follow the rule of one character per generation. Thus, the Taoists of Shanghai, Suchow, Mao Shan, Lung-hu Shan, south Fukien, and Taiwan, who received the Three Mountain transmission, do in fact use the character *Ting, Ta*, or *Luo* in their title, indicating a Sung dynasty origin to the alliance as stated above in note 13.

29. See Ch'en Yao-t'ing, in *Studies of Taoist Rituals and Music of Today* (ed.) Pen-yi Ts'ao (Hong Kong: Chinese University, 1989).

30. Michael Saso, *Chuang-lin Hsü Tao-tsang* (Taipei: Cheng-wen Press, 1975).

31. *Ibid.;* and Michael Saso, "The Structure of Taoist Liturgy." *Transactions of the International Conference of Orientalists in Japan*, 32 (Tokyo: Toho Gakkai, 1987), pp. 43-51.

32. The major "B" style liturgies are found in *Chuang-lin Hsü Tao-tsang*, sec. I, vols. 10-25, entitled *Ch'an* or *Ch'ing*.

33. *Ch'en Yao-ting* has shown that *P'u-tu*, which goes by other titles in mainland sources, is shared by the Taoists of Shanghai, Suchow, and Taiwan; see note 29 above.

34. Michael Saso, "The Chuang-tzu Nei-p'ien," *Experimental Essays on the Chuang-tzu* (ed.) V. Mair (Honolulu; University of Hawaii, 1983).

35. See the studies of Tanka Issei and Bartholomew Tsui, *Studies of Taoist Rituals and Music of Today* (ed.) Pen-yi Ts'ao (Hong Kong: Chinese University, 1989).
36. See John Lagerwey, *Taoist Ritual in Chinese Society and History* (New York and London: MacMillan, 1987) for an etic description of the *Chiao* festival.
37. The half-hour videotape "Rites of Origin: A Taoist Festival" (by Michael Saso, 1980) can be ordered through the University of Hawaii, Department of Religion, Honolulu, Hawaii, 96822. A Shanghai Academy of Social Sciences recording of the *Chin-piao* ceremony also is available. The author plans to videotape the Mao Shan and Lung-hu Shan *Chiao* in 1989-1990.
38. The Yellow Court Canon attributed to *Wei Po-yang*, and in its *Nei Chuan* form to the lady Taoist *Wei Hua-ts'un*, can be translated in three different ways: (1) physically, as sexual hygiene; (2) in the inner alchemy school as breath refinement; and (3) in the spiritual sense as union with the *Tao*. The *Shang-ch'ing* Mao Shan tradition and the Three Mountain Alliance use the manual only in the last sense, *i.e.*, as a manual for attaining union with the *Tao*. Sexual hygiene, or *Fang Chung*, the reader must be warned, does not belong to the classical monastic Taoist tradition, though many modern western versions of it do a brisk and profitable business in western languages as the "Tao of Sex." Sexual hygiene is considered heterodox to the celibate monastic traditions of the *Ch'uan-chen, Shang-ch'ing*, and the Three Mountain Alliance Taoists who go higher than Grade Six ordination. The Grade Five *Cheng-i Meng-wei* register and above preclude any notion of sex outside of wedlock for fire-dwelling Taoists and demand celibacy of the monastic orders.
39. *Lao-tzu*, chapter 42. The *Tao* gives birth to the One; here One signifies *T'ai-chi*, the Great First Principle. In the *Ho Shang Kung* commentary and later religious Taoist hermeneutics, *T'ai-chi* is equivalent to *Yüan-ch'i* (Primordial Breath). The *Tao* therefore gives birth to the Primordial Breath, the source of myriad creatures, as acted out in the *Fen-teng* rite during the *Chiao* ritual.

# BIBLIOGRAPHY

## Works from the Taoist Canon

*Ta-tung Chen Ching* [Highest Purity Great Receptacle of the True Canon]. The book is mentioned by *T'ao Hung-ching* in the *Chen Kao*, ca. the end of the fifth century. The version to be found in vols. 16-17 of the *Tao Tsang* has the signature of the 23rd-generation master of Mao Shan, Chu Tzu-ying, Sung dynasty. The book is a manual of meditations for instilling the spirits of the *Yellow Court Canon* into the body of the Taoist.

*Yüan-shih Wu-liang Tu-jen Shang-p'in Miao Ching* [Canon for Helping Men over the Difficult Stages of Life and Death]. TT 38-39. The *Tu-jen Ching*, the basic text whereby a Black-head Taoist lives, is first mentioned in the T'ang dynasty index of Taoist books. The version in TT 38-39 bears the signature of the Ch'i dynasty Taoist *Yen Tung* (ca. 479-501) and three T'ang dynasty Taoists. The commentary of *Ch'en Ching-yüan* dates from the Sung dynasty.

*Hsüan Tu Lü Wen* [Text of the Rules for a Taoist]. TT 78. Contains the rules for transmission of Taoist secrets. The book is first cited in the T'ang dynasty *San Tung Chu Nang*, TT 780-782.

*Tai Shang Huang T'ing Nei Ching Yü Ching, Wai Ching Yü Ching* [Yellow Court Canon, Esoteric and Exoteric Section—Canon and Supplement]. TT 168. Maspero (1950) holds that the *Wai Ching* is earlier than the *Nei Ching*, putting the latter between the fifth and seventh centuries. Cf. also TT 189, 190, and the *Yün Ch'i Ch'ien* vols. 11-12, TT 667-702. The *Yellow Court Canon* was mentioned in *Ko-Hung's* list of Taoist books in the *Pao-p'u-tzu*, published in 317 A.D.

*Teng Chen Yin Chüeh* [Secret Formula for Attaining Realization]. Compiled by the Liang dynasty Taoist *T'ao Hung-ching*, 452-536 A.D. TT 193.

*Ling-pao Ling-chiao Chi Tu Chin Shu* [The Ling-pao Liturgy, "Gold" Register]. 320 vols., TT 208-263. Collated by the Sung dynasty Taoist *Jan Ch'uan-chen*. The major rituals of the *Chiao* festival as I have described them (*e.g.*, *Su Ch'i, Fen Teng,* Three Audiences, etc.) are to be found in this collection.

*Wu-shang Huang-lu Ta-chai Li Ch'eng I* [Yellow Register liturgies]. 57 vols., TT 278-290. Some of the oldest specimens of Taoist liturgy are in this collection, including the *Su Ch'i* ritual in TT 281, ch. 16, bearing the signature of the Liang dynasty Taoist *Lu Hsiu-ching*.

*T'ai-shang Cheng-i Meng-wei Lu* or *T'ai-shang San-wu Cheng-i Meng-wei Lu*. TT 877. A list of the twenty-four registers with the sets of spirits which must be known by the grade four and five Black-head Taoist. The grade six Taoist knows the basic registers of this list in order to perform liturgy, particularly in order to perform the *Ch'u Kuan* rite at the beginning of each ceremony.

*T'ai-shang Cheng-i Meng-wei Fa Lu.* The fourteen registers which are the basic knowledge of the Red-head Taoists, or the *Shen-hsiao* order. A Red-head Taoist is thus called a *Meng-wei Fa-shih*, whereas a Black-head Taoist is a *San-wu Tu-kung.* TT 878.

*Shang-ch'ing Ling-pao Ta-fa* [A Treatise on Ling-pao Taoism]. TT 963-972. Perhaps the most helpful set in the Taoist canon for explaining Taoist liturgy and Taoist meditation, this collection of forty-four volumes was written by the Sung dynasty Taoist *Chin Yün-Chung* ca. 1220 A.D.

*Tao-men T'ung Chiao Pi-yung Chi* [Essential Rubrics for Taoist Ritual]. TT 984-985. Collated and commented on by the Sung Dynasty Taoist *Lü T'ai-ku.* The rubrics for the *Chin T'an* ritual are contained in great detail in ch. 7 of the collection.

*Cheng-i Hsiu Chen Lieh I* ["Orthodox One" Rites for Attaining Realization]. TT 990; anonymous. This text contains the twenty-four registers of the *San-wu Tu-kung*, and a description of the interior meditations going on during the liturgy. It also lists the days for Taoist meditation on the five primordial breaths.

The above is a list of texts directly cited from the Taoist canon in preparing my text. The sixth and seventh items, which contain a total of 377 titles, have been shortened in the general title of the collection. Works consulted but not cited are not included in the bibliography.

## Other Works in Chinese

Ch'en Kuo-fu, *Tao Tsang Yüan Liu K'ao* (Shanghai: Chung Hua Press, 1949).

Ch'en Kuo-fu, *Tao Tsang Yüan Liu K'ao*, 2 vols. (Peking: Chung Hua Press, 1963).

Koyanagi Shigeta, *Tao Chiao Kai Shuo* (trans.) Ch'en Pin-ho (Shanghai: Shang-wu Press, 1926).

*Ku wei shu.* Apocryphal Texts (Taipei: Wen-yu Press, 1968).

Lai Chih-te, *Lai Chu I-ching T'u Chieh* [Ming] (Taipei: I-chün Press, reprint, 1969).

Lao-tzu, *Tao-te Ching*, Kuo-hsüeh Chi-pen Ts'ung Shu (Taipei: Shang-wu Press, 1969).

*Li Chi*, Kuo-hsüeh Chi-pen Ts'ung Shu (Taipei: Shang-wu Press, 1969).

Liu An, *Huai Nan Hung Lieh Chi Chieh*, Kuo-Hsüeh Chi-pen Ts'ung Shu (Taipei: Shang-wu Press, 1969).

Liu Chih-wan, *Taipei-shih Sung-shan Ch'i An Chien Chiao Chi Tien* (Nankang, Taipei: Academia Sinica Monograph No. 14, 1967).

Liu P'ei-yüan (Liu I-ming), *I-tao Hsin-fa Chen-chuan*; Ch'ing, 1799, Ch'i yün Kuan (Taipei: Freedom Press, 1962).

Sung Yin-tzu, Shih Ho-yang, *Huang T'ing Wai Ching . . . (T'ai-shang Huang T'ing Ching Chu)*, Li Ming-ch'e P'ing (Peking: Pai-yün Shan Fang, 1794).

*Taiwan Sheng Tung-chih Kao*, Chuan Erh, *Tsung Chiao P'ien* (Taipei: Taiwan Wen-hsien Wei-yüan Hui, 1956).

Wang Ch'iung-shan, *I-hsüeh T'ung-lun* (Taipei: Kuang-wen Press, 1962).

*Wen Tao-tzu Chiang Tao Hua Lu* (Taipei: Chen Shan Mei Press, 1966).

## Works in Japanese

Fukui Kojun, *Dokyo no Kiso teki Kenkyu* [A Basic Study of Religious Taoism] (Tokyo: Shoseki Bunbutsu Ryutsu Kai, 1952). A scholarly treatment of the origins of religious Taoism.

Ikeda Toshio, *Taiwan no Ketai Seikatsu* [Family Life in Taiwan] (Taihoku: Toto Shoseki, 1944). A detailed study, with woodblock print illustrations, of household life and household beliefs in Taiwan.

Kataoka Iwao, *Taiwan Fuzoku, Meishin no Bu* [Taiwan Customs: Section on Superstitions] (Tainan: Taiwan-go Kenkyu kai, 1912). Pp. 48-64 on Taoism.

Kataoka Iwao, *Taiwan Fuzoku-shi* [A Book of Taiwanese Customs] (Taihoku: Taiwan Nichi-nichi Shinposha, 1920). One of the most complete ethnographies of pre-war Taiwan. Cf. esp. pp. 1058-1064 for the five kinds of Taoists.

Koyanagi Shigeta, *Ro-So no Shiso to Dokyo* [The Thought of Lao-tzu and Chuang-tzu and Taoism] (Tokyo: Morikita Shoten, 1942).

Kubo Noritada, *Dokyo Shiso no Hensen* [Changes in Taoist Thought] (Tokyo: Seikai-shi no Kenkyu, Yamakawa Shuppansha, 1965).

Kubo Noritada, *Junyokyu no Hekiga ni Mieru O Cho-yo Den* [Wang Chung-yang as Seen in the Drawings on the Walls of Ts'un-yang Kung] (Tokyo: Tokyo Daigaku, 1964).

Kubo Noritada, *Zenshinkyo no Seiritsu*, [The Founding of the Ch'uan-chen Sect] (Tokyo: Tokyo Daigaku, 1966).

Henri Maspero, *Le Taoïsme* (trans.) Kawakatsu Yoshio, *Dokyo, Fushi no Kenkyu* [Taoism, the Study of Immortality] (Tokyo: Tokai Daigaku, 1966).

Masuda Fukutaro, *Chugoku no Zoku-shin to Ho-shiso* [China's Popular Beliefs and Legalistic Mentality] (Tokyo: Sanwa Shobo, 1966).

Masuda Fukutaro, *Taiwan Honto-Jin no Shukyo* [The Religion of the People of the Island of Taiwan] (Tokyo: Meiji Shotoku Kinen Gakkai, 1935).

Masuda Fukutaro, *Taiwan no Shukyo* [The Religions of Taiwan] (Tokyo: Yoken-do, 1939).

Murakami Yoshimi, *Chugoku no Sennin, Ho-Boku-shi* [A Chinese Immortal, Pao-p'u-tzu] (Kyoto: Heiraku-ji, 1956).

Ofuchi Ninji *Dokyo-shi no Kenkyu* [Research on the History of Taoism] (Okayama: Okayama Daigaku, 1964). One of the most thorough and enlightened studies on the history of religious Taoism.

Michel Soymie, Yoshioka Yoshitoyo (ed.) *Dokyo Kenkyu* [Studies on Taoism] vol. II (Tokyo: Shoshin-sha, 1967).

Michel Soymie, Yoshioka Yoshitoyo (ed.) *Dokyo Kenkyu* [Studies on Taoism] vol. III (Tokyo: Toshima Shobo, 1968).

Suzuki Se-ichi-ro, *Kan-kon-so-sai to Nenchyu Gyoji* [Weddings, Funerals, and Annual Festivals of Taiwan] (Taihoku: Taiwan Nichi-nichi Shinpo-sha, 1934).

Takeuchi Sadayoshi, *Taiwan* [Taiwan] (Taihoku: Taiwan Kanko Kai, 1913). A massive ethnography of every phase of Taiwanese life.

Tseng Ching-lai, *Taiwan Shukyo to Meishin Roshu* [Taiwanese Religion and Rigid Superstitions] (Taihoku: Taiwan Shukyo Kenkyu Kai, 1938).

Yoshioka Yoshitoyo, *Dokyo Kyoten Shiron* [A Treatise on the History of Taoist Documents] (Tokyo: Taisho Daigaku, 1955).

## Works in Western Languages

Etienne Balazs, "La crise sociale et la philosophie politique à la fin des Han." *T'oung Pao*, 39 (1950) pp. 83-131.

Frederic Henry Balfour, "The Principle of Nature: A Chapter from the *History of Great Light*, by Huai-nan-tze, Prince of Kiang-Ling." *China Review*, 9, 5 (1880-81), pp. 281-297.

Wing-tsit Chan, *The Natural Way of Lao Tzu: A Source Book in Chinese Philosophy* (Princeton: Princeton University Press; London: Oxford University Press, 1963).

Wing-tsit Chan, "Taoism." *Encyclopedia Britannica* (Chicago, London, Toronto: 1960), vol. 21, pp. 796-797.

Wing-tsit Chan, *The Way of Lao Tzu: A Translation and Study of the Tao-te ching* (New York: Bobbs-Merrill, 1963).

Chung Yüan Chang, "The Concept of Tao in Chinese Culture." *Review of Religion*, 17 (1952-1953), pp. 115-132.

Chung Yüan Chang, *Creativity and Taoism: A Study of Chinese Philosophy, Art and Poetry* (New York: The Julian Press, 1963).

Edouard Chavannes, *Le T'ai chan: Essai de Monographie d'un Culte Chinois* (Paris: Annales du Musée Guimet. Bibliotheque d'études, 28, 1910), pp. 415-424.

Kenneth K.S. Ch'en, *Buddhism in China: A Historical Survey* (Princeton: Princeton University Press, 1964).

H. G. Creel, *Chinese Thought from Confucius to Mao Tse-tung* (Chicago: University of Chicago Press, 1953).

H. G. Creel, "What is Taoism?" *JAOS*, 76, 3 (1956), pp. 139-152.

James Davidson, *The Island of Formosa* (London, 1903).

Henri Doré, *Laotse et le Taoisme: Recherches sur les Superstitions en Chine* (Shanghai: Zi-ka-wei Press, 1920), tome 18.

Homer H. Dubs, "Taoism." *China* (ed.) Harley Farnsworth MacNair (Berkeley and Los Angeles: University of California Press, 1946), ch. 17, pp. 266-289.

Wolfram Eberhard, *Guilt and Sin in Traditional China* (Berkeley: University of California Press, 1967).

Han-chi Feng, "The Origin of Yü Huang." *HJAS*, 1 (1936), pp. 242-250.

Raleigh Ferrell, *Taiwan Aboriginal Groups: Problems in Cultural and Linguistic Classification* (Taipei: Academia Sinica, 1969).

Yu-lan Fung, *A History of Chinese Philosophy* (trans.) Derk Bodde (Peking: Henri Vetch, 1934), vol. I.

Yu-lan Fung, *A History of Chinese Philosophy* (Princeton: Princeton University Press and London: G. Allen & Unwin, 1952-1953), vol. II.

Yu-lan Fung, *Lao Tzu and Chuang Tzu: The Spirit of Chinese Philosophy* (trans.) E. R. Hughes (London: Kegan Paul, 1947).

Yu-lan Fung, *A Short History of Chinese Philosophy* (ed.) Derk Bodde (New York: MacMillan, 1948).

Peter Goullart, *The Monastery of Jade Mountain* (London: J. Murray, 1961).

A. C. Graham, *The Book of Lieh-tzu: A New Translation* (London, 1960).

Marcel Granet, *La Pensée Chinoise* (Paris, 1934).

Marcel Granet, *La Religion des Chinois* (Paris, 1922).

J. J. M. de Groot, *Les Fêtes Annuellment Célèbrées à Amoui* (Amoy), *Étude Concernant la Religion Populaire des Chinois* (Paris: Annales du Musée Guimet, Bibliotheque d'études, 12, 1886), pp. 691-706.

J. J. M. de Groot, *On the Origin of the Taoist Church* (Oxford: Transactions of the 3rd International Congress for the History of Religions, 1908), vol. I.

J. J. M. de Groot, *The Religious System of China* (Leiden, 1892-1910), 6 vols.

J. J. M. de Groot, *Sectarianism and Religious Persecution in China* (Amsterdam, 1903).

Edward Herbert, *A Taoist Notebook* (London: Wisdom of East Series, 1955; New York: Grove Press, 1960).

Max Kaltenmark, *Lao Tseu et la Taoïsme* (Paris, 1965; English ed., Stanford: Stanford University Press, 1969).

Max Kaltenmark, "*Le Taoïsme*": *Aspects de la Chine* (Paris: Publications de Musée Guimet, Bibliotheque de Diffusion, 1959), vol. I, pp. 151-160.

Max Kaltenmark, "Ling-pao: Note sur un Terme du Taoïsme Religieux." *Mélanges Publies par l'Institut des Hautes Études Chinoises*, 2 (Paris: Bibliotheque de l'IHEC, 14, 1960), pp. 559-588.

Max Kaltenmark, "Notes à propos du Kao-mei EPHE." *Sc. R. Annuaire* (1966-1967), pp. 5-34.

Carl F. Kupfer, *Sacred Places in China* (Cincinnati: Western Methodist Press, 1911).

D. C. Lau, *Lao Tzu: Tao te Ching* (Baltimore: Penguin Books, 1963).

James Legge, *The Religions of China: Confucianism and Taoism Described and Compared with Christianity* (London, 1880).

James Legge, *The Tao teh king, or the Tao and Its Characteristics: The Sacred Books of the East* (ed.) F. Max Müller, vol. XXXIX. *The Texts of Taoism* (London: Oxford University Press, 1891), pp. 45-124 (plus introduction, pp. 1-44); second impression, London, 1927. New edition (New York: The Julian Press, 1959).

Howard S. Levy, "Yellow Turban Religion and Rebellion at the End of the Han." *JAOS*, 76, 4 (1956), pp. 214-227.

Henri Maspero, "Les Procédés de Nourrir le Principe Vital dans la Religion Taoïste Ancienne." *JA*, 229 (1937), pp. 177-252, 353-430.

Henri Maspero, "Le Taoïsme." *Mélanges Posthumes sur les Religions et l'Histoire de la Chine*, 2 (Paris: Publications de Musée Guimet. Bibliotheque de Diffusion, 58, 1966).

Paul Michaud, "The Yellow Turbans." *MS*, 17 (1958), pp. 47-127.

Evan Morgan, *Tao, The Great Luminant: Essays from Huainan tzu.* (London: Kegan Paul, 1933).

Joseph Needham, "The Tao Chia (Taoists) and Taoism: Chin and Thang Taoists." *Science and Civilisation in China: History of Scientific Thought* (Cambridge: Cambridge University Press, 1956), vol. 2.

Michael Saso, *Taiwan Feasts and Customs* (Hsinchu, Taiwan: Fu Jen University Language School Press, 1965).

Kristofer M. Schipper, "The Divine Jester: Some Remarks on the Gods of the Chinese Marionette Theater." *Bulletin of Institute of Ethnology* (BIE). Academica Sinica, No. 21 (Spring, 1966).

Kristofer M. Schipper, *L'Empereur Wou des Han dans la Legende Taoïste* (Paris: Publications de l'École Française d'Extreme-Orient, 1965).

Kristofer M. Schipper, "Le Wou-yue tchen-hing-t'ou et son Culte." *Études Taoïstes* (Tokyo: Shoshinsha, 1967).

Anna Seidel, *La Divinisation de Lao-Tseu dans le Taoïsme des Han* (Paris: Publications de l'École Française d'Extreme-Orient, 1969).

Vincent Y. C. Shih, "Some Chinese Rebel Ideologies." *TP*, 44, 1-3 (1956), pp. 150-226.

William Edward Soothill, *The Three Religions of China: A Study of Confucianism, Buddhism and Taoism* (London: Hodder and Stoughton, 1913).

R. A. Stein, "Remarques sur les mouvements du Taoisme politico-religieux au II^e^ siècle après J. A." *TP*, 50, 1-3 (1963), pp. 1-78.

Laurence G. Thompson, *Chinese Religion: An Introduction* (Belmont, California: Dickenson Publishing Co., 1963).

Arthur Waley, *Three Ways of Thought in Ancient China* (London: G. Allen & Unwin, 1939).

Arthur Waley, *The Way and Its Power* (London: 1934; Boston: Houghton Mifflin, 1935).

James R. Ware, *Alchemy, Medicine and Religion in China of A.D. 320: The Nei-p-ien of Ko Hung (Pao-p'u-tzu).* (Cambridge: Massachusetts Institute of Technology, 1966).

James R. Ware, *The Sayings of Chuang Chou* (New York: New American Library, 1963).

James R. Ware, "The Wei shu and the Sui shu on Taoism." *JAOS*, 53 (1933), pp. 215-250; 54 (1934), pp. 290-294.

Burton Watson, *Basic Writings of Chuang Tzu* (New York: Columbia University Press, 1964).

Max Weber, *Taoism, The Religion of China: Confucianism and Taoism* (trans. and ed.) Hans H. Gerth (New York: Free Press, 1951).

Holmes Welch, "The Bellagio Conference on Taoist Studies." *History of Religions*, IX, 2-3 (1969-1970), pp. 107-136.

Holmes Welch, "The Chang t'ien shih and Taoism in China." *JOS*, 4 (1957-1958), pp. 188-212.

Holmes Welch, *The Parting of the Way, Lao Tzu and the Taoist Movement* (Boston: Beacon Press, 1957).

Leon Wieger, *Histoire des Croyances Religieuses et des Opinions Philosophiques en Chine depuis l'Origine jusqu'a Nos Jours* (Hien hien: 1917, 1922, 1927; Paris: 1953).

Leon Wieger, *Lao-tzeu: Textes Philosophiques, Confucianisme, Taoïsme, Bouddhisme* (Ho-kien fou: Imprimerie de la Mission Catholique, 1906).

Leon Wieger, *Tao-te-king, l'Oeuvre de Lao-tzeu: Taoïsme.* t. 2 *Les Peres du Système Taoiste* (Hien hien (Ho-kien fou): 1913; Paris, 1950).

C. K. Yang, *Religion in Chinese Society* (Berkeley: University of California Press, 1961).

Ying-shih Yü, "Life and Immortality in the Mind of Han China." *HJAS*, 25 (1964-1965), pp. 80-122.

E. Zürcher, *The Buddhist Conquest of China: The Spread and Adaptation of Buddhism in Early Medieval China* (Leiden, 1959).

# Works Published after 1970

Donna Au and Sharon Rowe, "Bibliography of Taoist Studies." *Buddhist and Taoist Studies I* (ed.) Michael Saso, David W. Chappell (Honolulu: University of Hawaii Press, 1977).

Charles D. Benn, "Taoism as Ideology in the Reign of Emperor Hsüan-tsung (712-755)." Ph.D. diss., University of Michigan, Ann Arbor, 1977.

Stephen R. Bokenkamp, "Sources of the Ling-pao Scriptures." *Tantric and Taoist Studies in Honor of R. A. Stein* (ed.) Michel Strickmann (Brussels, 1983), pp. 434-486.

Judith Boltz, "Opening the Gates of Purgatory: A Twelfth Century Taoist Meditation Technique for the Salvation of Lost Souls." *Tantric and Taoist Studies in Honor of R. A. Stein* (ed.) Michel Strickmann (Brussels, 1983), pp. 488-510.

Judith Boltz, *A Survey of Taoist Literature* (Berkeley: University of California, 1987).

Alfredo Cadonna, *l'Taoista di sua maesta* (Venice: Libreria Editions Cafoscarina, 1984).

Fukui Kojun, *Dokyo* [Taoism], 3 vols. (Tokyo: Hirakawa Shuppansha, 1983).

Norman J. Girardot, *Myth and Meaning in Early Taoism: The Theme of Chaos* [Huntun] (Berkeley: University of California, 1983).

Angus C. Graham, *Chuang-tzu, The Seven Inner Chapters* (London: George Allen and Unwin, 1981).

Hisayuki Miyakawa, "Local Cults Around Mt. Lu at the Time of Sun En's Rebellion." *Facets of Taoism* (ed.) Holmes Welch, Anna Seidel (New Haven: Yale University Press, 1979), pp. 83-101.

Rolf Homann, *Pai Wen P'ien, or the Hundred Questions* [A dialogue between two Taoists on the macrocosmic and microcosmic system of correspondences] (Leiden: E.J. Brill, 1976).

Hou Chin-lang, "The Chinese Belief in Baleful Stars." *Facets of Taoism* (ed.) Holmes Welch, Anna Seidel (New Haven: Yale University Press, 1979), pp. 193-228.

Jan Yün-hua, "The Religious Situation and the Studies of Buddhism and Taoism in China, an Incomplete and Imbalanced Picture." *Journal of Chinese Religion*, 12 (1984), pp. 37-64.

John Keupers, "A Description of the Fa-ch'ang Ritual as Practiced by the Lü Shan Taoists of Northern Taiwan." *Buddhist and Taoist Studies I* (ed.) Michael Saso, David W. Chappell (Honolulu: University of Hawaii Press, 1977), pp. 79-94.

Kubo Noritada, *Chugoku no Shukyo Kaikau, Zenshin Kyo no Seiritsu* [China's Religious Reformation: the Founding of the Ch'uan-chen Taoist Movement] (Kyoto: Hozokan, 1967; 1988 revision).

Kubo Noritada, *Dokyo no Hyakka, Sennin e no Akogare* [Taoist Sayings, the Yearning for Immortality] (Tokyo: Shoten Kanko Shakai, 1983).

Kubo Noritada, *Dokyo no Kamigami* [Taoist Spirits] (Tokyo: Hirakawa Shuppansha, 1986).

Kubo Noritada, *Dokyo Nyumon* [An Introduction to Taoism] (Tokyo: Nanto Shobo, 1983).

Kubo Noritada, *Dokyo Shi* [The History of Taoism] (Tokyo: Yamakawa Shuppansha, 1977).

John Lagerwey, *Taoist Ritual in Chinese Society and History* (New York and London: MacMillan, 1987).

John Lagerwey, *Wu-shang pi-yao, somme Taoïste du VIe siècle*, [École Française d'Extreme Orient] vol. 124 (Paris, 1981).

Liu Chih-wan, *Chung-kuo Min-chien Hsin-yang Lun-chi* [A Treatise on Chinese Folk Beliefs] vol. 22 (Taipei: Academia Sinica, 1974).

Liu Ts'un-yan, *New Excursions into the Hall of Harmonious Wind* (Leiden: E. J. Brill, 1983).

Liu Ts'un-yan, *Selected Papers from the Hall of Harmonious Wind* (Leiden: E. J. Brill, 1976).

Liu Ts'un-yan and Judith Berling, "The 'Three teachings' in the Mongol-Yüan Period." *Yüan Thought: Chinese Thought and Religion Under the Mongols* (ed.) Theodore de Bary, Hok-lam Chan (New York: Columbia University Press, 1982), pp. 479-512.

Piet van der Loon, *Taoist Books in the Libraries of the Sung Period: A Critical Study and Index* (London: Ithaca Press, 1984).

Lu Gwei-djen, "The Inner Elixir [Nei-tan]: Chinese Physiological Alchemy." *Changing Perspectives in the History of Science: Essays in Honor of Joseph Needham* (ed.) M. Teich, R. Young (London: Heinemann, 1973), pp. 68-84.

Henri Maspero, *Taoism and Chinese Religion* (trans.) F. Kierman (Amherst: University of Massachusetts, 1981).

Joseph Needham, Lu Gwei-djen, "Facets of Taoism." *Science and Civilization in China*, vol. 5, part V (Cambridge: Cambridge University Press, 1983).

Ofuchi Ninji, *Chugokujin no Shukyo Girei* [Chinese Religious Ritual, a Study of the Chiao Ritual of Master Ch'en, Tainan City, south Taiwan] (Tokyo: Fukutake Shoten, 1983).

Ofuchi Ninji, "The Formation of the Taoist Canon." *Facets of Taoism* (ed.) Holmes Welch, Anna Seidel (New Haven: Yale University Press, 1979), pp. 253-267.

Ofuchi Ninji, "On the Ku Ling-pao Ching [The Ancient Ling-pao Canon]," *Acta Asiatica*, 27 (1974), pp. 34-56.

Ofuchi Ninji, *Tonko Dokyo: Mokuroku-hen* [Index of Taoists Texts in the Dunhuang Collection] (Okayama: Okayama University, 1978).

Duane Pang, "The P'u-tu Ritual: A Celebration of the Chinese Community of Honolulu." *Buddhist and Taoist Studies I* (ed.) Michael Saso, David W. Chappell (Honolulu: University of Hawaii, 1977), pp. 95-112.

Pen-yi Ts'ao (ed.) *Studies of Taoist Rituals and Music of Today* (Hong Kong: Chinese University, 1989).

Isabelle Robinet, *La révélation du Shangqing dans l'histoire du taoïsme*, [École Française d'Extreme Orient] vol. 137 (Paris, 1984).

Isabelle Robinet, *Les commentaires du Tao-tö king jusqu'au VIIe siècle*, Memoirs de IHEC, 5 (Paris: College de France, 1982).

Isabelle Robinet, *Meditation taoïste* (Paris: Dervy-livres, 1979).

Isabelle Robinet, "Randonées extatiques des taoïste dans les astres." *Monumenta Serica*, 32 (1976), pp. 159-273.

Michael Saso, *Chuang-lin Hsü Tao-tsang*, 25 vols. [The Chuang-Lin Supplement to the Taoist Canon] (Taipei: Cheng-wen Press, 1975) [Rites and rubrics of renewal, burial, and exorcism].

Michael Saso, "The Chuang-tzu Nei-p'ien." *Experimental Essays on the Chuang-tzu* (ed.) V. Mair (Honolulu: University of Hawaii, 1983).

Michael Saso, "Classification of Taoists According to the Documents of the 61st Celestial Master." *Bulletin of the Institute of Ethnology*, vol. 30, 2 (Tapei: Academia Sinica, 1972), pp. 69-82.

Michael Saso, *Dokyo Hiketsu Shusei* [A Collection of Taoist Esoteric Texts] (Tokyo: Ryukei Shosha, 1978-1979).

Michael Saso, "On the Ling-pao Chen-wen." *Toho Shukyo* (Tokyo, 1977).

Michael Saso, "On the Su-ch'i Liturgy: the Structure of Taoist Ritual." *Symposium on Taoist Music* (Hong Kong: Chinese University, 1988).

Michael Saso, "On the Yellow Court Canon." *Journal of the China Society*, 9 (1974), pp. 1-23.

Michael Saso, "Orthodoxy and Heterodocy in Taoist Ritual." *Religion and Ritual in Chinese Society* (ed.) A. Wolf (Stanford: Stanford University Press, 1974), pp. 325-336.

Michael Saso, "Religion in the People's Republic," *China News Analysis* (Hong Kong, December 15, 1987).

Michael Saso, "Seito Dokyo no Denjyu Kyokai." [On the Classical Making of a Taoist Priest] *Toho Shukyo* (Tokyo: 1975), pp. 15-33.

Michael Saso, "The Structure of Taoist Liturgy." *Transactions of the International Conference of Orientalists in Japan*, 32 (Tokyo: Toho Gakkai, 1987), pp. 43-51.

Michael Saso, *The Teachings of Taoist Master Chuang* (New Haven: Yale University Press, 1978).

Michael Saso, "What is the Ho-t'u?" [The Use of Wei-apocryphal Texts in the Classical Taoist Tradition] *History of Religions*, vol. 17 (Chicago: University of Chicago, 1979).

Michael Saso, David W. Chappell (ed.) *Buddhist and Taoist Studies I* (Honolulu: University of Hawaii, 1977).

Edward Schafer, "The Jade Woman of the Great Mystery." *History of Religions*, 17 (1978), pp. 387-398.

Edward Schafer, *Mao Shan in T'ang Times*. Society for the Study of Chinese Religions, Monograph 1 (Boulder, 1980).

Edward Schafer, *Pacing the Void: T'ang Approaches to the Stars* (Berkeley: University of California, 1977).

Edward Schafer, "The Restoration of the Shrine of Wei Hua-ts'un at Lin-ch'uan in the Eighth Century."

Kristofer M. Schipper (ed.) [concordances published by the École Française d'Extreme Orient, Paris]: *Concordance du Tao-tsang*, vol. 102 (1977); *Concordance du Houang-t'ing king*, vol. 103 (1975); *Index du Yunji qiqian*, vol. 131 (1981-1982). [Concordances compiled by Li Mei-chin, Ch'en Min-chu, Ch'eng Yü-chao, *et al.*].

Kristofer M. Schipper, *Le corps taoïste* (Paris: Librairie Arthème Fayard, 1982).

Kristofer M. Schipper, *Le Fen-teng: rituel taoïste*, EFEO, vol. 102 (Paris, 1975).

Kristofer M. Schipper, "Vernacular and Classical Ritual in Taoism." *Journal of Asian Studies*, 45 (1985), pp. 21-57.

Gary Seaman, "Chinese Shamanism and the Emperor of the Dark Heavens." Ethnographic videotape of a Taiwanese *Tang-ki* performance with mimeographed notes, 1984.

Anna Seidel, "Imperial Treasures and Taoist Sacraments—Taoist Roots in the Apocrypha." *Tantric and Taoist Studies in Honor of R. A. Stein* (ed.) Michel Strickmann (Brussels: 1983), pp. 291-371, with 287 references summarizing the works of Strickmann, Schipper, and Yasui Kozan.

Anna Seidel, "Le sutra merveilleux du Ling-pao Suprème." *Contributions aux étude de Touen-houang* (ed.) M. Soymie (Paris, 1984), pp. 305-352.

Anna Seidel, Hubert Durt, John Lagerwey (ed.) *Cahiers d'Extreme Asie* [École Française d'Extreme Orient]: vol. I (1985), vol. II (1968), vol. III and IV (1988-1989).

Nathan Sivin, "On the Word *Taoist* as a Source Perplexity." *History of Religions*, vol 17 (Chicago, 1978), pp. 303-330.

Nathan Sivin, "Report on the Third International Conference on Taoist Studies." *Society for the Study of Chinese Religions Bulletin*, 7 (1979), pp. 1-23.

Michel Soymie (ed.) *Contributions aux études de Touen-houang* (Geneva and Paris: Librairie Droz, vol. 1-3, 1979, 1981, 1984).

Rolf Stein, "Religious Taoism and Popular Religions from the Second to the Seventh Centuries." *Facets of Taoism* (ed.) Holmes Welch, Anna Seidel (New Haven: Yale University Press, 1979), pp. 53-81.

Michel Strickmann, "History, Anthropology, and Chinese Religion." *Harvard Journal of Asian Studies* (1980), pp. 201-248.

Michel Strickmann, "The Longest Taoist Scripture." *History of Religions*, vol. 17 (Chicago, 1978), pp. 331-354.

Michel Strickmann, "The Mao Shan Revelations: Taoism and the Aristocracy." *T'oung-pao* 63 (1977), pp. 1-64.

Michel Strickmann, "On the Alchemy of T'ao Hung-chiung." *Facets of Taoism* (ed.) Holmes Welch, Anna Seidel (New Haven: Yale University Press, 1979), pp. 123-192.

Michel Strickmann, "Sodai no raigi: Shinsho undo to Doka nanshu ni tsuite no ryakusetsu." [Sung Thunder Rites: The Shen-hsiao Movement and the Taoists of the Southern Sung] *Toho Shukyo*, 46 (Tokyo, 1975), pp. 15-28.

Michel Strickmann (ed.) *Tantric and Taoist Studies in Honor of R. A. Stein* (Brussels, 1983).

Sun K'ok'uan, "Yü Chi and Southern Taoism During the Yüan Rule." (ed.) J. Langlois, *China Under Mongol Rule* (Princeton, 1981), pp. 212-253 [Based on 1965 and 1968 studies in Chinese.]

Tadao Sakai (ed.) *Dokyo no sogoteki kenkyu* [Proceedings of the Second International Conference on Taoist Studies] (Tokyo: Kokusho Kankokai, 1977).

Tadao Sakai, Noguchi Tetsuro, "Taoist Studies in Japan." *Facets of Taoism* (ed.) Holmes Welch, Anna Seidel (New Haven: Yale University Press, 1979), pp. 269-287.

Holmes Welch, Anna Seidel (ed.), *Facets of Taoism* (New Haven: Yale University Press, 1979).

Yoshioka Yoshitoyo, "Taoist Monastic Life." *Facets of Taoism* (ed.) Holmes Welch, Anna Seidel (New Haven: Yale University Press, 1979), pp. 229-252.

Yoshioka Yoshitoyo, *Eisei e no Negai* [The Quest for Eternal Life] (Tokyo: Tankosha, 1970).